ᴓ **After**
Buddhism
a workbook

After Buddhism
a workbook

Winton Higgins
with Jim Champion and Ramsey Margolis

TUWHIRI

Wellington

Aotearoa New Zealand

First published 2018

The Tuwhiri Project
PO Box 6626
Wellington 6141
Aotearoa New Zealand
www.tuwhiri.nz

The authors and The Tuwhiri Project would like to thank all our
Kickstarter donors for their generosity; without you this book
would not exist

ISBN 978-0-473-44517-1

A catalogue record for this book is available from the
National Library of New Zealand
Kei te pātengi raraunga o Te Puna Mātauranga o Aotearoa te
whakarārangi o tēnei pukapuka

Design John Houston
Cover montage main photo: Chicago from a helicopter
by Patrick Tomasso on Unsplash
Set in Fira Sans and IBM Plex Serif
Printed in Aotearoa New Zealand

10 9 8 7 6 5 4 3 2 1

For all those who seek to live well

℘ Contents

Foreword   ix

Preface   x

Session one   What is *After Buddhism* all about?   1

Session two   After Buddhism   5

Session three   Mahānāma the convert   15

Session four   A fourfold task   25

Session five   A fourfold task, sections 7 & 8   33

Session six   Pasenadi, the king   41

Session seven   Letting go of truth   49

Session eight   Sunakkhatta the traitor   57

Session nine   On experience   63

Session ten   Jīvaka the doctor   71

Session eleven   The everyday sublime   81

Session twelve   Doubt and imagination   87

Session thirteen   Ānanda the attendant   95

Session fourteen   A culture of awakening (part 1)   103

Session fifteen   A culture of awakening (part 2)   111

Session sixteen   Ten theses of secular dharma   119

References   112

The authors   125

About The Tuwhiri Project   126

After Buddhism, *a workbook*

℘ Foreword

After Buddhism: rethinking the dharma for a secular age is the culmination of more than forty years' study and practice of the Buddha's teaching. The book weaves together various ideas and themes that have engaged me as a practitioner and writer throughout this time. This process has been an ongoing struggle to articulate the dharma in a contemporary language stripped of the metaphysical and cosmological views of ancient India. It has likewise been a continuous attempt to divest the dharma of the trappings of dogma and priestly authority that continue to characterise the Buddhist religion. In hindsight, I see this work as part of a wider movement towards an unashamedly secular vision of what the Buddha taught.

I am most grateful to Winton Higgins for developing and teaching his study course on *After Buddhism,* which has now resulted in this workbook. I hope that this volume will not only deepen your understanding of what *After Buddhism* is about, but also encourage you to examine the text critically, thereby enabling you to become 'independent of others' in your own practice of being human. Many thanks also to Jim Champion for contributing the discussion questions and to The Tuwhiri Project for making this book available.

Stephen Batchelor
Aquitaine, April 2018

∅ | Preface

You have decided to study Stephen Batchelor's *After Buddhism: re-thinking the dharma for a secular age*. Excellent! His book explores early Buddhism anew, and expresses its profound meaning and practice in terms relevant to the circumstances we encounter in the twenty-first century.

His main title signals a critique of *conventional versions* of 'Buddhism' that the west has received from long-established Asian institutions and teachers. These versions typically embody unappealing cultural sensibilities, assumptions and exclusions that mask the burning relevance of the tradition's early teachings for today's westerners in particular. In short, Stephen seeks to retrieve the early teachings and apply them to the lives we lead now. He's by no means suggesting that the dharma itself is superseded.

This workbook builds on a sixteen-session study course based on *After Buddhism* presented by Winton Higgins to two Sydney *sanghas* (practice communities – Bluegum and Golden Wattle respectively). It follows the same sixteen sessions as the study course, which in turn reflects the chapter-structure of Stephen's book. The course and this workbook divide some of the weightier chapters of *After Buddhism* into two sessions.

More than a few participants from both sanghas offered the suggestion that the course should be made more widely available.

Hence this workbook, which is intended to underpin both group and individual study. For maximum benefit, *After Buddhism* and the workbook can be read together. The discussion questions that conclude each session have been contributed by Jim Champion and are intended to stimulate both group discussion and individual reflection.

Readers will find a selected list of references at the back of this book. It lists books and other source that the main text explicitly or implicitly cites.

We are deeply grateful for Stephen Batchelor's encouragement, to everyone who backed us on Kickstarter, and to John Houston in London for designing the cover and the pages of this workbook.

If you have any questions about *After Buddhism* or about this workbook, write to ask@tuwhiri.nz.

Winton Higgins, Sydney
Jim Champion, Southampton
Ramsey Margolis, Wellington
April 2018

∅ Session one: What is *After Buddhism* all about?

Stephen faced the difficulty common to all book authors – what to call the damn thing. A book title has to convey an instant message, and situate that message in relation to all the other books current in its subject area. Following advice from his editor, he followed today's conventional wisdom: give the book a grabby 'generic' title, followed by a subtitle that is more informative. Hence *After Buddhism: rethinking the dharma for a secular age*.

In choosing this title, he has followed (among others) Gianni Vattimo, the post-metaphysical philosopher who chose to remain a Catholic, though on an idiosyncratic basis, and called his book exploring this choice *After Christianity*. In both cases, what is being superseded is a conventional conception of a tradition which offers riches now buried beneath outmoded or inappropriate ways of expressing and practising it.

In this context, we should remember that the concept and term 'Buddhism' was an early-nineteenth century European invention. As far as I know it has no equivalent in any Asian language, and certainly not in the tradition's classical languages – Pali, Sanskrit, Chinese and Tibetan. So we can tease out Stephen's main title to mean something like, 'after we get beyond today's conventional understanding of what Buddhism is, including the idea that it stands for just one monolithic tradition'. Taken as a whole, his title counterposes this 'Buddhism' with the living dharma tradition that Gotama (c. 480–400 BCE), 'the historical Buddha', founded in the Ganges Basin in northeastern India.

The project heralded by the subtitle, *rethinking the dharma for a secular age*, almost certainly contains an implicit reference to the development of secular Christianity over the past half-century. In his preface, Stephen mentions among his principal sources of inspiration the progressive Protestant theologians Paul Tillich and Don Cupitt, who were in much the same business of rethinking Christianity for our secular age.

The issues for both traditions converge. On this point you are invited to jump onto the web and go to the transcript of a public dialogue, organised in 2012 by London Insight Meditation, between Stephen Batchelor and Don Cupitt – one moderated by *Guardian* journalist Madeleine Bunting. It's available online at http://secularbuddhism.org/2012/08/02/batchelor-cupitt/.

Here Don Cupitt – after 50 years as an Anglican priest – talks about Jesus as a first-century CE humanistic, radical, and this-worldly teacher whose message was mystified and mythologised by 'the first clergymen', Peter, James and Paul, around 50 CE. It didn't take long! (As we'll see, it didn't take long in the case of the dharma either.) Thereafter ecclesiastical Christianity developed, with its social conservatism, and its other-worldly and supernatural preoccupations.

To rethink Christianity for a secular age means to start with what was actually on the table before the 'clergymen' turned up. This is not to reject anything useful the many generations of clergymen have developed over the centuries, but it does uncover the foundations of the living tradition, and thus honours that tradition in the best possible way – an intelligent, sceptical one.

The parallel with the dharma is striking. The Buddha too was a grounded, radical, this-worldly existential teacher, but the 'clergy-men' (or professionals, with Kassapa in the lead) quickly arrived on the scene after his death and took the tradition off into other-worldly realms, metaphysical beliefs, elaborate institutions, and ritualism. Once again, the challenge for those wanting to practise the dharma as a living tradition is to attempt to go back to the source as the founder left it, and from there figure out how to apply it in our own secular age, noting useful contributions that others have made in the intervening time.

So Stephen's book isn't a secular Buddhist polemic, still less an attempt to establish a new orthodoxy. Rather, it's a fresh investigation of what the big and untidy Pali canon actually contains. It's a new extrapolation, one driven by the central question the dharma poses (to use the traditional Ch'an formulation): how are we to confront 'this great matter of life and death'? How are we to viscerally understand our lives as vulnerable, mortal beings endowed with consciousness? How do we make these lives meaningful and dignified – fully human? How are we to maximally occupy the human estate?

Stephen expresses his own search more simply and personally: 'As a practicing Buddhist, I look to the discourses not just to mine them for scholarly knowledge but to come to terms with my own birth and death' (p.21).

In *After Buddhism*, he presents us, among other things, with a fresh approach to mining the canon. One aspect of his approach consists in highlighting those teachings that are uniquely the Buddha's own, and not simply drawn from the culture of his time and place, such that any contemporary spiritual teacher might have uttered them. A second aspect of Stephen's approach takes the form of following the stories of some of the canon's more interesting characters. The early dharma isn't solely populated with standardised saintly re-nunciants – there are busy lay people like us in it too, and some of them were relatives and close friends of the Buddha.

These people faced major exigencies in their daily lives and their inner psychological tangles, but nevertheless gained the Buddha's accolade of 'seers of the deathless'. That is, at least some of the time, they dwelled in a sensibility permeated by the insight into condi-tionality ('dependent arising') and the experience of not-self. Their interactions with him and his feedback to them are extraordinarily poignant. They tell us much about how the dharma suffuses an ordinary human life to make it extraordinary.

And so we meet Mahānāma (the Buddha's cousin who, under dif-ficult circumstances, became the chief of the small Sakiyan republic – a position formerly held by the Buddha's father, Suddhodana); Pasenadi (the king of Kosala); and Jīvaka (the physician at the Maga-dhan court). Such people performed vital communal functions, and the way the Buddha counselled them reflects his own conception of a healthy community and a good society.

Here we can get a sense of the dharma practitioner's civic role. All this sets up a contrast to conventional Buddhism's preoccupation with the serene monastic who spurns political and other worldly engagements in pursuit of individual salvation. In a similar vein, Stephen homes in on *the experience of conversion* to the dharma and the never-ending challenge of cultivating a way of life that nurtures its values. In one case of a monk we meet here, Sunakkhatta, the transition turns out to be too great, and he jumps ship.

Does a secular approach to dharma practice militate against re-ligion? he asks. Not if you accept Paul Tillich's idea of what religion is basically about – pursuing some 'ultimate concern', such as the existential questions above.

As noted above, Stephen's ultimate concern encompasses the existential questions that arise as he comes to terms with his own birth and death. In his account, the Buddha offers four central, unique ideas to guide this project: his 'four Ps':

- The *principle* of conditionality
- The *practice* of a fourfold task
- The *perspective* of mindful awareness
- The *power* of self-reliance' (p.27)

Right. Let's get started.

Questions for study

1. How would you respond to someone who asks with genuine curiosity: 'Are you a Buddhist?'

2. How do you feel about Stephen's approach to the Pali canon: gleaning those of the Buddha's pronouncements that were uniquely his own, as opposed to ones that any teacher at the time might have uttered?

3. Where have you looked in order to come to terms with your own birth and death?

4. Have you ever had to rethink something from the ground up? How did it go?

5. How useful (or indeed possible) is it to try to go back to the start of something that has such a long history, such as Buddhism?

6. Do the introductory remarks about a secular approach to religion resonate with you? If so why? And if not, why not?

∅ Session two:
After Buddhism

In this session we'll look at the first chapter of Stephen's book, also called 'After Buddhism'. Here he unfurls his intention with this book and the inquiry it undertakes. In the introductory session, we situated Stephen's book title in a group of books with titles beginning with 'After': Gianni Vattimo's *After Christianity*, Don Cupitt's *After God* (both texts by Christian intellectual 'relatives' of Stephen), and the 2014 essay collection, *After mindfulness* edited by his Zen friend, existential psychotherapist Manu Bazzano. In all four cases, the implication of the 'after' is: once we get beyond conventional, habitual, institutionalised and unexamined versions of the subject matter in question.

In the latter stages of the chapter, Stephen names his project as an exploration of a *secular Buddhism* which, he writes, 'would seek to return to the roots of the tradition and then rethink and re-articulate the dharma anew' (p.19). Part of the 'return' aspect is to mine the early teachings as they were before 'the first clergymen' began fiddling with them and overlaying them with institutionally on-message re-workings, additions and commentaries.

The 'rethinking and re-articulating' part refers to maximising the *usefulness and applicability* of these teachings for inhabitants of 'the secular age' with our this-worldly orientation, scepticism, and our reality-construct based on evolutionary biology, big-bang theory, neuroscience, etc. For those of us who aren't too time-poor and have a philosophical bent, Charles Taylor's 741-page book *A secular age* would make an excellent companion volume. The two principal points that Taylor makes are that:

- secularity and religion aren't mutually exclusive, especially since secularity is a product of the long-run religious-cultural development in the west; and
- in religious terms, our secular age arises from *'changed conditions of belief'*: we no longer believe – nor can even make sense of – hand-me-down myths, and supernatural and metaphysical assertions. Thus each of us has to take responsibility for what we choose to believe, knowing that there are plenty of alternative ways of seeing – knowing that none of us can claim possession of absolute truth.

Stephen's take on a secular Buddhism

Stephen's secular Buddhism seeks to reinvigorate the dharma as a *living tradition,* and so he distances himself energetically from two related quasi-secular *subversions* of the tradition today:

- The move 'to discard all traces of religiosity, that seeks to arrive at a dharma that is little more than a set of self-help techniques that enable us to operate more calmly and effectively as agents or clients, or both, of capitalist consumerism'. This includes a mindfulness industry that 'reinforces the solipsistic isolation of the self by immunising practitioners against the unsettling emotions, impulses, anxieties, and doubts that assail our fragile egos' (p.17). Among other things, this secularising tendency 'disenchants' the world, whereas Stephen seeks to 're-enchant' it by restoring a sense of wonder, perplexity and the sublime in everyday life; and

✍ The offering (and marketing) of Buddhist practices and ideas in a way that makes them palatable for 'those who have no interest in committing themselves to the core values of the dharma' (p.17).

Stephen's secular Buddhism would be much more radical than such manifestations because, as an *ethical* undertaking, it would infuse all aspects of our lives and resist compartmentalisation.

One issue we might take with him touches on his presentation of earlier laicisation and modernisation of Buddhism as also representing a secular tendency. The most pertinent example he names is the vipassanā schools, which arose in the late nineteenth century in Burma, Sri Lanka and Thailand as a form of resistance to Protestant Christian missionary incursion.

The schools' founders tore two leaves out the Protestants' playbook: making texts available to the laity (including in vernacular languages), and upgrading and dignifying lay practice. Protestantism was itself a harbinger of modernity, and the vipassanā schools' 'Protestant Buddhism' certainly stood for modernisation and a degree of laicisation. But otherwise they preserved the conventional teachings, hierarchies and institutions of pre-existing Buddhism.

Certainly in terms of western secular development, I'd prefer to stick with Taylor here: secularity was a slowly growing element in western religious culture for around seven centuries, but has really only flowered in 'the secular age' from the 1960s onwards. Not so incidentally, this was the decade when secular Christianity first appeared, and when Ñāṇavīra penned arguably the first secular Buddhist text: *Clearing the path* (first published in 1987).

Scepticism and pragmatism
Let's go back to the beginning of the chapter: Stephen quotes the

Buddha as he remarks on the intense controversies between opposing metaphysical beliefs abroad in the spiritual marketplace of his time and place. People who engage in those sorts of arguments are blind, the Buddha says: '*They do not know what is of benefit and what is of harm.* They do not understand what is and what is not the dharma.'

Fast forward 2,300 years and we find pragmatist philosophers shocking their colleagues by adopting this criterion. A good idea is one that is *useful and beneficial,* not one that can claim to be correspond with some version or other of ultimate reality. The Buddha immediately goes on to suggest that his dharma rests on precisely this claim to usefulness, not ultimate truth.

This is the suck-it-and-see (*ehipassiko*) dharma, not something that is 'right' rather than 'wrong'. When asked, 'What are the teachings of an entire lifetime?', Zen patriarch Yunmen (10th century CE) replies: 'An appropriate statement.' At first this reply might sound like just another bit of cryptic Zen zaniness. But think about it. When someone close to you finds herself in a crisis – from the dishwasher breaking down mid-cycle to a sudden personal tragedy – how would you want your years of dharma practice to manifest in that moment? Yunmen is on the money, isn't he? The last thing your friend needs is a smart-arse analysis of her predicament, however profoundly true you may think it is.

Conventional Buddhism insists that it possesses, and is partly defined by, metaphysical truth claims – such as the doctrine of rebirth – irrespective of their usefulness and plausibility in modern culture. For instance, Ajahn Brahmavamso – a prominent western-born monk who's gone out on a limb to support women's ordination – has banned all dharma teachers who fail to affirm rebirth *in writing* from teaching at the Buddhist Society of Victoria. Starting with Stephen Batchelor! Clearly the dharma itself means entirely different things to these two veteran Buddhist practitioners.

The Buddha saw a lot of this sort of thing in his own time. He once compared the dharma to a venomous snake. You must know how to grasp it properly, he suggests, otherwise it can do you a lot of harm. How does Stephen suggest we grasp it?

Situating the dharma

We must situate the dharma on the *common ground* all human beings share, he writes. Of course, this starts with our being conditioned, mortal and vulnerable beings endowed with consciousness, which leads to our common experience of 'unknowing, wonder and perplexity' (p.4). The dharma is about living on this common ground, and attending to this common experience, in the most skilful and meaningful way possible – in a way that leads us into another experience within our reach: *awakening*.

Stephen reminisces about his first seven years as a dharma practitioner, spent in the Geluk school of Tibetan Buddhism. It was 'an intact medieval Buddhist world', complete with beliefs most of us would now find bizarre; but it also immersed him '*in a refined culture of awakening*' (p.4). For this reason, it offered him an invaluable grounding in the dharma. If the dharma is anything, it is a *culture of awakening*, with all that that implies (sometimes uncomfortably for us hyper-individualistic westerners) for *communality* and the refuge of sangha life.

The leitmotif of this culture, as Stephen received it from his first mentors and has stuck with ever since, concerns *emptiness*. That is, the visceral realisation of the absence of 'something that had never been there in the first place', namely, existence independent of shifting conditions.

The various ways in which emptiness has been taught tells a story about how doctrinal approaches have tended to distort the original meaning of emptiness. In the Mahāyana schools, emptiness (*shunyata* in Sanskrit) is a big metaphysical concept that began life more humbly, in the Buddha's teaching, as 'not-self' (*anattā* in Pali). But the Buddha himself once spoke of *sunya* ('emptiness' in Pali) in a snippet of dialogue with Ananda, who asked him if it was true that he 'mainly dwelled by dwelling in emptiness'. The Buddha replies: that's right.

So here emptiness is a metaphorical *abode*, a dwelling place where one can live. It is, Stephen writes, 'a perspective, a sensibility, a way of being in this poignant, contingent world... emptiness discloses the dignity of a person who has realized what it means to be fully human' (p.7). It has nothing to do with cracking open some esoteric truth, thus going *beyond* suffering, or the human condition in general. Rather, it's a way of deepening into the human condition by leaving reactivity behind.

'The point is not to understand emptiness but to *dwell* in it. To dwell in emptiness brings us firmly down to earth and back to our body.' And so Stephen comes to 'one of the key questions' he'll pursue in the book: 'How... did the concept of emptiness evolve from a way of dwelling on earth unconditioned by reactivity, into an ultimate truth...?' (p.10).

Contrary to that evolution, the path of practice leads not to certainty, but to its opposite: an encounter with uncertainty, doubt, existential questioning, and 'the everyday sublime' (a phrase that we'll unpack in session 11). A good guide here is the Korean Sŏn practice of meditating on the question: *What is this?* One asks this question with the whole body, 'its 360 bones and joints, and the 84,000 pores of one's skin' (p.11).

Community, sangha

For the Buddha, the vehicle of this culture of awakening was an egalitarian, gender-inclusive community (*sangha*) of both mendicants (beggars, renunciants) and adherents (laity, the non-professionals). Needless to say, conventional Buddhism supports an organisational culture quite at odds with this model – one that sets monastics above the laity, and subordinates and marginalises women.

A vital part of the secular-Buddhist agenda must be to return to the Buddha's model of sangha, which also satisfies the requirements of today's progressive precepts for how we should associate with one another as dharma practitioners.

Questions for study

1. Take a look at the list of various conflicting beliefs and opinions taught by the priests, wanderers and ascetics who lived in the Buddha's time near Jeta's Grove, set out on pp.1–2 of *After Buddhism*: the world is/is not eternal; the world is/is not finite; body and soul are identical; body and soul are different; an enlightened one exists/does not exist after death; an enlightened one both exists and does not exist after death; an enlightened one neither exists nor does not exist after death. Which, if any of these, would you say that you believed, and how would you justify your belief (if any)? Are there any that you used to believe, but have now changed your mind about? If so, what led to you changing your mind?

2. At the end of section 2, Stephen writes that he cannot pretend that his rethinking of the dharma has not been deeply influenced by the culture in which he was raised. To what extent do his life circumstances match your own? How might the similarities and/or differences influence your own assessment of Stephen's rethinking of the dharma?

3. Midway through section 3, Stephen describes emptiness as disclosing the dignity of a person who has realised what it means to be fully human. How would you recognise someone who had realised what it means to be fully human, someone who is 'dwelling in emptiness'?

4. To what extent do you endorse the ways that Stephen uses the words 'religious' and 'secular'? What issues, if any, have you encountered in your life in relation to these two terms?

5. What is this?

℘ Session three:
Mahānāma: the convert

Chapter two of Stephen's book, 'Mahānāma: the convert', brings together some central themes to do with the primacy of conversion to the dharma, and what practice and community in this tradition entail. These issues arise out of the story of Mahānāma, the Buddha's cousin and chosen chief of the Sakiyans, their shared political community.

From the conventional Buddhist viewpoint, Mahānāma is a contradictory figure, which may well explain why conventional commentaries ignore him – in spite of the several significant references to him in the Pali canon. He is no renunciant. Rather, he's a busy man of the world, caught up in the affairs of his worldly community and the irrepressible desires of the flesh, at the same time plagued by existential angst and fear of death. And yet he enjoys the Buddha's acknowledgement as a 'stream enterer' – one whose conversion to the dharma is complete.

Thus he has '*lucid confidence*' (not blind faith, you'll note) in the Buddha, dharma and sangha, and he 'possesses the virtues dear to the noble ones', all of which imbues him with spiritual dignity. He thus fulfils the Buddha's four criteria for stream entry (*sotāpatti*).

Not only that, either. The possession of these four attributes means he 'slants, slopes and leans' towards nirvana, that is, towards a state of mind that overcomes reactivity. This quality earns

Mahānāma another accolade from the Buddha: he is 'a seer of the deathless', where death itself is a metaphor for a life lived in the thrall of unreflective and habitual reactivity.

From a conventional point of view, a 'worldling' like him could never attain stream entry. Yet here he is, stream entry certified by the Buddha himself. In this way he becomes a person of interest as we work through some fundamental issues about what dharma practice is all about.

Concrete lives in concrete settings

One of the shortcomings of conventional presentations of the Buddha's life is the suppression of its concrete context in favour of mythologising it, for instance by presenting him as a prince of the royal blood in a settled society. But in the present chapter we get a sense of the turbulence in which the Sakiyans (the Buddha and his cousins included) were embroiled during the agricultural revolution on the Ganges plain.

Mahānāma would dearly love to embrace the serenity of the mendicant life, but he feels a civic duty to steer his compatriots through very troubled waters indeed, running the risk of assassination in the process. He laments the physical danger his situation keeps him in, in terms that might remind us of Shakespeare's famous line in *Henry IV*, part II, 'Uneasy lies the head that wears a crown.'; even if the 'crown' in this case is a republican one. For someone in his shoes, the life of a mendicant wanderer with a begging bowl and not a care in the world would be far preferable. But in the end he dies on the job, as a hero trying to deflect a genocidal attack on his people by Kosalan forces.

Another interesting point that modern scholarship has unearthed is this: the Sakiyans were animist sun-worshippers. They weren't under the thrall of Brahminism with its belief system and rigid social divisions, including between women and men. Brahmin communities and wanderers were known to them, and dominant in neighbouring areas, but that's all.

The Buddhadharma defined itself *against* Brahminism from time to time, but coming out of Sakiya, it didn't constitute a *rebellion against it*. This fact explains the sun-imagery in the Pali canon: like the sun, the dharma illuminates and animates a life that would otherwise unfold in darkness and torpor. This is something that goes to the core of what conversion and stream entry mean.

Conversion and stream entry

In conventional (especially Theravādin) Buddhism, stream entry refers to an advanced *meditative experience* that confers a hierarchical status on an (almost invariably) monastic practitioner. It is a rank that one *attains*: the lowest of four ranks in the 'noble community' (*ariyasangha*), a rank from which one progresses to once-returner, non-returner, and finally, a fully awakened *arahant*. The *ariyasangha* conventionally refers to all who have had the first serious meditative awakening experience.

This progression is similar to that in the army, from brigadier to major-general, to lieutenant-general, to the top rank – field marshal. Based on his experiences as a monk, Jason Siff's satirical novel, *Seeking nibbana in Sri Lanka*, depicts the obsession around attainment of stream entry in monastic circles there.

But in the Buddha's own world and usage, these terms had quite other meanings. The 'stream' metaphor refers to a free-flowing, un-obstructed way of being in the world. A stream flows freely because it is held in place by banks on either side which guide it and hold it. The banks refer to dharma practice, and especially its ethics. How does one 'enter the stream'? As for any old body of running water, one does so by locating oneself between those banks.

That means conversion in the sense already mentioned: gaining 'lucid confidence' in the Buddha, dharma and sangha, and living a coherent ethical life. It means embracing a perspective and a way of life *that was not previously known*, 'which transcended the parochial concerns of family and tribe and inspired him to live according to a universal set of values,' Stephen writes (p.48). A synonymous metaphor for this stream is the eightfold path.

Stream entry thus has nothing to do with a special kind of meditative experience; it simply (but significantly) refers to an existential turning point, a re-orientation that immediately admits the new adherent to the noble community, the *ariyasangha* consisting of *all* those who have turned the same corner. It even includes the town drunk, Sarakāni, according to the Buddha.

Conversion and stream entry together represent *the* crucial moments in dharma practice. They set us up for glimpses of *nirvana* – that is, a taste of what it means to live without reactivity. So nirvana is not some sort of end goal or status either. Rather, it's an experience (however fleeting): a marker, like the ones you sometimes see when walking in a national park. They reassure you that you're on course.

So what is an *adherent*? Mahānāma asks the Buddha. The Buddha's answer, as Stephen comments, serves to describe dharma adherents in our own time as well: an adherent is one who has gone for refuge to the Buddha, dharma and sangha; abstains from killing, stealing, sexual abuse, lying and intoxicants; has faith in the Buddha's own awakening; and 'dwells at home with a mind devoid of stinginess, freely generous, open-handed'; and 'possesses understanding directed to arising and ceasing, which is noble and penetrating' (p.47). The latter implies a firm grip on contingency (conventionally called 'dependent arising') and impermanence.

Pinning down what 'adherent' means may lead us to wonder what the other alternative, 'mendicant' entails. Wandering mendicants were common on the Ganges plain in the Buddha's day. They followed – or were themselves – teachers of many different stripes, and had renounced the 'household life'. They followed many different disciplinary codes, or none at all. In a pragmatic way, the Buddha bit-by-bit developed a code (the *vinaya*) for his own mendicant followers. He made the rules up to cover problems as and when they arose.

As Stephen points out, this scenario is a far cry from the big, solid monastic institutions that would come along later. So the adherent/mendicant distinction in the Buddha's time was only an instrumental one; it shouldn't be equated with the heavy-duty *religious* contrast that subsequently attached to the lay/monastic dichotomy. Adherents and mendicants entered the same stream, cultivated the same eightfold path, participated in the same community.

And note the nice *balance between community and individuality* that comes across in this chapter. The Buddha emphasised that the practitioner must 'make the path her own', be able to practice 'independent of others'. And yet the practice is a communal one in all its aspects. The community is the bedrock on which the individual cultivates her own authentic individuality.

Mahānāma's issues

Stephen opens this chapter with Mahānāma's worry that, if he were to die suddenly – in an accident or attack – his state of mind at the point of death might be a long way from the dharma, and he'd then suffer an unfortunate rebirth. Some conception of rebirth conditioned by one's mind state at the point of death was common coin in the Buddha's time and place, and conventional Buddhism perpetuates it. We see the same worry in conventional Catholicism: the afterlife can be pretty grim if a priest doesn't come to your deathbed and administer extreme unction before you draw your last breath, let alone if you're not even baptised.

The Buddha's answer to his cousin gives such technical (not to say superstitious) belief short shrift. What matters is how we develop as human beings throughout our lives, which he compares to the angle at which a tree grows. If we take charge of our underlying development, we have nothing to fear from the incidental circumstances surrounding our death.

But Mahānāma displays a wider weakness here: his fear, and his corresponding craving for certainty, which has the potential to turn him into a dogmatist, a fanatic. It makes it difficult for him to enter into the uncertainty and perplexity which (as we saw in the last session) inheres in the dharmic view of the human condition.

He also tends to be torn between the lusts of the flesh on the one hand, and the subsequent regrets (self-punishment) on the other. These two are dead-ends, the Buddha tells him; he must learn to pass freely between them. We can make a cross-reference here to the Buddha's first discourse, which begins with the description of the path as avoiding the dead ends of addiction to sensuality and addiction to self-mortification.

More generally, the stream flows freely when it encounters no obstacles – the obstacles of reactivity that inhibit the flow and create turbulence.

Personal salvation or a new civilisation?
Given all the points that the Buddha made to and about Mahānāma, we may sense that dharma practice is not so much about some arduous individual path that eventually leads a few full-time *religiosi* to personal sanctity and salvation, but rather a way of being in the world that people in general can share and cultivate.

This idea is something altogether new ('*not previously known*' as the Buddha put it). It offers its adherents a coherent, ethical, contemplative and philosophical approach to living their lives and to relating to one another. This approach lifts them out of the dead end of repetitive, unreflecting, parochial existence, and brings them into touch with universal values, such that they enter fully into the human estate.

As Stephen writes, 'Gotama's dharma opened the door to an emergent civilisation rather than the establishment of a "religion".' (p.48).

Questions for study

1. In his 1854 work, *Walden; or, life in the woods,* the American poet Henry David Thoreau wrote:

> The millions are awake enough for physical labor; but only one in a million is awake enough for effective intellectual exertion, only one in a hundred millions to a poetic or divine life. To be awake is to be alive. I have never yet met a man who was quite awake. How could I have looked him in the face?

As a 'seer of the deathless', do you think Thoreau could have looked Mahānāma in the face? What can we learn about our attitude towards awakening from contemplating this question?

2. Whatever your current circumstances, how tempted are you by the prospect of living a serene mendicant life? Have you ever felt drawn towards such an existence? To what extent do you think that the idea of being a mendicant – a wanderer with a begging bowl – has been romanticised?

3. In the world of conventional Buddhism, stream entry is usually presented as induction into an exclusive club. On what grounds is membership granted, and who ensures that non-members are kept out? How fair is this analogy? Can the same analogy be applied to Stephen's presentation of stream entry as an existential turning point?

4. In what sense was the adherent/mendicant distinction an instrumental one? How did it differ from the later lay/monastic distinction in Buddhist traditions?

5. Mahānāma's concerns about his mind state at the point of death may well seem overly orthodox or superstitious to you. But do you have a more modern worry about not living up to strict criteria? Do you engage in unhelpful behaviour out of a fear of facing uncertainty – behaviour that an objective observer might see as a dharmic 'dead end'? How would taking charge of your underlying development as a human being help you to pass freely between such dead ends?

6. To what extent do you think that the Taoist sentiment, 'the path is the goal', sits comfortably with Stephen's interpretation of dharma practice?

∅ Session four:
A fourfold task

Chapter three of *After Buddhism* is called 'A fourfold task'. It takes up central issues about what the dharma is, its thrust, and how it is to be practised. You'll remember the subtitle of the book, 'rethinking the dharma for a secular age'. Well, compared to conventional renderings, this chapter honours the subtitle quite intensely. While you may be familiar with aspects of its interpretation, there are altogether new elements here as well.

The material in this chapter is too rich to devour in one sitting, so we'll hold over the last part, on the path, from section 7 (p.83), until the next session.

'Our place' and 'this ground'

Let's start with the Buddha's own earliest account of his awakening, in the quote from the teaching on 'the noble quest' in the canon, at p.55 of *After Buddhism*:

> This dharma I have reached is deep, hard to see, difficult to awaken to, quiet and excellent, not confined by thought, subtle, sensed by the wise. But people love their place (*ālaya*): they delight and revel in their place. It is hard for people who love, delight and revel in their place to see this ground (*thāna*): "because-of-this" conditionality (*idappaccayatā*), conditioned arising (*paticcasamuppāda*).

And also hard to see this ground: the stilling of inclinations, the relinquishing of bases, the fading away of reactivity, desirelessness, ceasing, nirvana.

There are many terms here that call for unpacking, but the standout feature is the tension and contrast between two terms that almost seem to mean the same thing: 'place' and 'ground'. Our 'place' can refer quite literally to our home, but expands out from there to encompass all that is familiar to us, that defines us, that locates us, that constitutes our identity. Here we have our family, our occupation, our habitual pastimes, our habitual reactions, and our endlessly rehearsed views about our world. This is the place we 'love ... delight and revel in,' the Buddha says.

And because we're so trapped in it, we can't '*see*' the dharma, '*this ground*': the alternative perspective. This ground is another base, or basis, for being-in-the-world. This ground rests on two supports: *conditionality* (variously called 'dependent arising' or contingency); and nirvana in the sense we explored in the previous session: the ceasing of reactivity.

To practise the dharma is to develop, by degrees, 'this ground' as our main perspective on being-in-the-world. Making 'this ground' our own doesn't involve uncovering esoteric truths or conversion to another set of beliefs, but rather finding our feet on this ground, and so becoming a more developed human being, a different kind of self.

Stephen quotes a pithy verse from the *Dhammapada* which compares *self*-development with a farmer irrigating a virgin field, a fletcher fashioning an arrow and a woodworker shaping an object. Each of us is an unfinished project, a work in progress, and will ever remain so. (Forget about perfectionist hang-ups – they're not where dharma practice is at!)

We'll never abandon our 'place' entirely – we'd cease to be human if we did. There are important values to be cultivated as participants in the daily round, in what Freud summarised as *love* and *work* – the two critical components of a life well lived.

Probably the Buddha himself always remained the individual called Gotama, with all that this identity implied. But his main dwelling was on 'this ground', the dharmic perspective characterised by causality/contingency, impermanence, compassion and equanimity.

'Place' and 'ground' don't constitute an either/or. But the path of practice leads us to adopt 'this ground' as our *home perspective*, our default setting, as that which illuminates and transforms our lives in 'our place'. It's a radical new way of reconfiguring the lives we're already living.

Stephen compares 'this ground' with a sudden clearing in a thick forest, a place of unobstructed vision where we can see what enables and what inhibits human flourishing. Among other things, we can see that responsiveness, not reactivity, should be the mainspring of our engagement with our world.

Nirvana

What of nirvana, the second aspect of 'this ground'? It might well be one of the most mystified words in our language – meaning 'heaven' in popular parlance, and a remote and mystical state of grace in the conventional Buddhist tradition. For the Buddha it's nothing of the sort. He describes it as 'immediate, clearly visible, inviting, uplifting and personally sensed by the wise,' (p.59), that is, accessible to us all – at least on a good day. He describes it in the same terms as the dharma itself. It simply refers to those moments (however fleeting) of lucidity and serenity when we've freed ourselves from all reactivity.

Why does this original sense of nirvana strike us as so surprising

now? After the Buddha's death, the tradition became institutionalised, and thereby reinterpreted, in a 'Brahmanised' way, Stephen
explains. Brahmanism (the first draft of Hinduism) is a classic religious *soteriology*: it holds out the prospect of salvation, of redemption,
in the form of a ticket to a radically and permanently altered form of
existence – another *plane* of existence altogether, a superhuman or
beyond-human one. Nirvana has been made to serve as the prom-
ised land beyond this human vale of tears.

This whole idea is completely at odds with the thrust of dharma
practice as the Buddha taught it, which was about *human* flourishing (in Greek, *eudaimonia*). Nirvana stands for the acme of human
flourishing. We'll come back to this point later, when we look at the
implications of the eightfold path.

The fourfold task

You may be aware of the revision of the 'four noble truths', the cen-
trepiece of conventional Buddhism, to become the four great tasks.
This line of interpretation began with Ñanavīra Thera's work in
the early 1960s, and has culminated in Stephen's teaching, backed
up by the scholarship of the Pali linguist, Kenneth Norman. Quite
simply, the Buddha's first discourse did not announce any 'truths'
at all, 'noble' or otherwise. What the discourse does crucially do is
set out the four *tasks* with which dharma practice begins.

Dharma practice is a question of tackling tasks, not believing 'truths'.

This chapter of *After Buddhism* contains an enriched and updated version of the teaching of the four tasks. In it, we find the tasks
themselves to be so tightly sequential as to constitute just one task
with four identifiable facets or moments. The four great tasks thus
become the fourfold task. Let's now briefly revisit the first three of
the four moments of the dharmic task, and deal with the last in the
next chapter.

1. *Dukkha* is to be comprehended – totally known (*pariññā*)

Dukkha is conventionally translated as 'suffering', which would fit the soteriological element in conventional Buddhism. But it's quite incapable of expressing the Buddha's explicit list of what dukkha stands for: birth, sickness, ageing, death, separation from what we love, being stuck with what we detest, not getting what we want, and our overall psychophysical vulnerability. No human being can evade any of these experiences.

So this first facet of the fourfold task is about *embracing our human condition*. This life also includes pleasure, and the potential for awakening, the Buddha taught. But the way to an enhanced experience of these boons lies in coming to grips with 'the whole catastrophe', as Zorba the Greek put it.

We don't need esoteric knowledge to comprehend dukkha. We need the ethical and meditative *know-how* to embrace life 'intimately and ironically with all its paradoxes and quirks, its horror and jokes, its sublimity and banality,' Stephen writes (p.73).

2. Arising (*samudaya*) is to be let go of (*pahāna*)

It's entirely natural for us humans to react to our constantly shifting environment. We're hardwired to do that. This is what 'arising' refers to: 'the myriad reactions that life provokes in us'. These reactions are evolutionary factors: back in our old cave-person days they underwrote our survival.

But they get out of hand: *reactivity* (in the Buddha's words) 'is repetitive, wallows in attachment and greed, obsessively indulges in this and that: craving for stimulation, craving for existence and craving for non-existence'. And it gets worse: we tend to ruminate on all this stuff, we *proliferate* it, we *cling* to it. We become 'like tangled balls of string', as the Buddha colourfully puts it (p.76).

We need to recognise the pattern. And we need to let go of reactivity – know it, and step back from it, the second facet of the fourfold task admonishes. If we do that, what happens? We move on to the third facet.

3. Ceasing (*nirodha*) is to be beheld (*sacchikāta*)

Here comes the nirvana moment: in the Buddha's words, 'the traceless fading away and ceasing of that reactivity (*taṇhā*), the letting go and abandoning of it, freedom and independence from it' (p.79). This experience doesn't call for a life of renunciation, highly developed technical meditation skills, or even a male rebirth in aid of monkhood. It is – as we've already seen – 'immediate, clearly visible, inviting, uplifting, and personally experienced by the wise'.

The trick here is this: to *turn up* for the experience, to be *alert* for it, and to know it for what it is – to *behold* it. We need to 'consciously affirm and valorise those moments when you see for yourself that you are free to think, speak, and act in ways that are not determined by reactivity. Nirvana is a space of moral possibility, the gateway to an ethical life,' Stephen writes (p.80).

Another (Chinese) way of putting it is that the nirvana moment is a *dharma door* to be entered in full confidence. Where does it take us? Onto the eightfold path, the final facet of the fourfold task. Which we'll cultivate in the next session.

The overcooked, mystical account of nirvana obscures its vital function in the fourfold task, which is to propel us onto the path, as we'll see next time.

Questions for study

1. The verse from the *Dhammapada* about the farmer, the arrowsmith and the carpenter 'are drawn from the life of daily toil in a community of farmers and artisans'. Suggest equivalent images drawn from your own modern-day community, and evaluate how well your images help to convey the concept of the individual as always being 'an unfinished project, a work in progress'.

2. How does the concept of a person as a 'work in progress' fit with the messages about personhood and maturity that you heard throughout your own upbringing? As a child did you have the impression that adults were finished people? Do you live your life as if there is some point in the future when you'll be 'complete'?

3. Can you acknowledge the likely reasons for your behaviour when you are primarily concerned with your place in the world? Stephen mentions examples such as maintaining your place in society, enhancing your status in the workplace, or improving your handicap at golf. How difficult do you find it to get a perspective of greater objectivity on your own motivations? Could you perhaps seek feedback on this point from a trusted friend who is willing to be frank with you?

4. 'Clearly visible', yet 'hard to see' – what is your understanding of this tension?

5. 'To detest one's place only to delight in another does not, from Gotama's point of view, solve anything. Without a genuine change of heart in one's core relationship to one's life as it is, pursuing a "spiritual" vocation will be a waste of time.' Have you seen this fruitless pursuit in others: your parents, your friends, your children, in celebrity figures? To what extent do you see it in your own life trajectory?

6. Stephen writes that, 'The Buddha is aware that these forces [of reactivity – "Mara's army"] cannot be excised by performing a kind of spiritual lobotomy.' What do you think he means by the term 'spiritual lobotomy'? How comfortably could you use this kind of terminology within the 'spiritual' circles in which you move?

7. How do you feel about the translation of dukkha as 'suffering'? Have you heard other translations that have made more or less sense to you than the English word 'suffering'?

℘ Session five:
A fourfold task, sections 7 & 8

In this session we're looking at sections 7 and 8 of chapter three, 'A fourfold task', of Stephen Batchelor's *After Buddhism*. These sections deal with the eightfold path, and where it leads. The path is the fourth 'fold' of the fourfold task – Stephen's retrieval of the teaching in the Buddha's first discourse. In conventional Buddhism, this teaching is presented as the 'four noble truths'. For reasons given in the previous session, we replace it with the teaching of the four tasks, or alternatively the fourfold task.

In that previous session we also reviewed the first three folds of the task – or if you prefer, the first three of the four great tasks: embracing *dukkha*; letting go of the reactivity that naturally arises in us (in the form of craving, aversion and confusion); and stopping and *savouring* the cessation of reactivity. This third task refers to nirvana – those at first fleeting moments, glimpses, when we become aware that all reactivity has ceased, and we're at peace.

To recap the main points in the earlier parts of this chapter: the Buddha drew a contrast between two perspectives – one ('our place') based on clinging to our familiar world, the other ('this ground') based on a vision of:

℘ **conditionality**, and all that it implies: roughly, the three characteristics of conditioned existence: impermanence, dukkha, and not-self; and

☞ **nirvana** – the experience of the cessation of reactivity. The Buddha described this experience as immediately accessible and inviting.

We have to abide in both perspectives: they are not alternatives. But dharma practice will shift our centre of gravity to the dharmic 'ground'.

The exposition of the fourfold task shows that the Buddha's foundational teaching was about doing, not believing. What we are doing – in formal meditation, and in living mindfully – is saying 'yes' to *life in its entirety*, including the difficult bits, and in *this way* not falling for (letting go of) the unhelpful escape route of reactivity. And then, savouring the deep peace and wisdom of a mind free of reactivity.

That experience of nirvana, however momentary, is one of confidence in the practice, a dharma gate onto the wholehearted cultivation of the path. By cultivating the path we expand the fourfold task into a coherent way of life. A life that is integrated and grounded, rather than showy and pious. A life that *makes sense*.

The eightfold path

Stephen translates the Pali adjective *sammā*, as it qualifies each fold of the path, literally: as 'complete'. So the path consists in cultivating complete view, thought, speech, action, livelihood, effort, mindfulness, and concentration (or 'mental integration', which is closer to the literal meaning). In a moment we can tease out some of these 'folds' (or 'branches', as Stephen calls them).

First, though, we need to ponder the word 'path' (*magga*) itself. We usually think of a path as a clearly defined way from A to B that we can stroll down with ease. But the verb attached to it here is the all-important *bhāvanā*, 'to cultivate'. We don't say: 'I think I'll just cultivate the path from Sydney Hospital across the Domain to the art gallery and check out its new exhibition.' Clearly something much more demanding is implied by the word 'cultivate'. Cultivation requires ongoing care and focus. As in horticulture or agriculture, we can't expect a good harvest without sustained care and commitment beforehand.

The **second** overarching aspect of the path we need to note is that it's a formula for an *ethical life*. It expresses the dharma's fundamental values, both in their entirety, and in concentrated form in the 'speech', 'action', and 'livelihood' branches. Once again, note the distinction between an *ethical* and a *moral* system.

Ethics, in particular situational ethics, is about fundamental values, commitment to which often requires us to make tough judgements on the basis of sensitivity to unique situations and the likely *consequences* of each alternative choice available to us. Morality or legalistic ethics, by contrast, typically takes the form of rules to be dutifully obeyed in all situations, such as: 'Thou shalt rest on the sabbath day'; and: 'Thou shalt not covet thy neighbour's BMW nor their significant other'. Following a situational ethical path demands much more awareness and wisdom from us.

The **third** point to notice is the logical order in which the 'branches' are named. This is no shopping list, but rather a flow chart. By re-ordering the way we perceive our self and our world, we can rework our thoughts and intentions, and so tackle the fundamental issues about how we manifest in the world and interact with all it contains.

But the flow chart extends itself into a feedback loop. The last three folds mainly concern our approach to meditation – what we *glean* from our careful and conscious participation in the world, which helps us to reinforce, refine and complete our 'view' when we loop back to the top of the list.

Starting at the top, with complete view

What is 'complete view'? Evidently (from our discussion of 'place' and 'ground') the view from 'our place' – our familiar inner and outer world referred to earlier – is an *incomplete* view. But it is the view that everyday language reflects. So we say, for instance, 'This is my house,' and 'This is not my dirty linen.' All very cut and dried.

In this way we become 'bewitched' (in Wittgenstein's term) by the appearance of things as couched in our familiar language. It creates a mutual-reinforcement society of 'me' and 'my house': I gain a solid sense of my identity through ownership of 'my house'; and it becomes a solid, enduring entity through its relationship to Me.

But the view from 'this ground', by contrast, goes beyond every-day language and is quite different, as it's based on impermanence, dukkha and not-self, for starters. Neither I nor my house has any inherent existence: we simply arise and pass away according to shifting conditions – we are more like events than entities. As Shakespeare put it in *The Tempest*, 'All that is solid melts into air.'

'Complete view' must also embrace the view from 'this ground', then. It takes focus and effort, and quite a bit of courage, to culti-vate it. When the Buddha was explaining the problem to Kaccāna, he said that 'this world is bound to its prejudices and habits' – its unexamined assumptions, stereotypes, and other habits of mind. Or, in the Buddha's words: 'habits, fixations, prejudices or biases of the mind' (p.85).

To cultivate the view from 'this ground', we must not only careful-ly observe the way in which supposedly solid things aren't so solid after all ('my house' keeps falling into disrepair, and so do 'I'), but also probe our sneaky assumptions and belief systems.

Yet we need the view from this ground to subvert our reactivi-ty. Here we're moving into the territory of branch two of the path: 'complete thought'. The neighbour's BMW might cost a fortune to insure against all manner of contingencies, and to service and repair; and their significant other looks like a bit of a flight risk. Potential heartache all round, really. (Dukkha is a great teacher!) So non-attachment and contentment seem like good options. In this way, 'complete thought' extends to appropriate intention, which in turn invokes the directly ethical branches of the path (three, four and five), covering speech, action and livelihood.

The conventional Buddhist wisdom (often repeated in the introduction to retreats) is that you need a strong ethical basis for your meditation practice. Apart from its other essential functions, a sound ethical life settles the jittery static of life, and calms and steadies us to turn our gaze inwards. Such is the subliminal message we get from the placement of the meditation branches (six through eight) of the path (energy, mindfulness, integration) after the overtly ethical ones.

Where does the path lead?
The religification of the dharma left it as a common or garden doctrine of personal salvation or redemption: a soteriology. Within this lifetime, or in some future one, we're to attain individual enlightenment, which is a one-way ticket to some blissful realm or other. Bye bye dukkha!

That is not how the Buddha himself presented it. You may be familiar with the parable of the ancient city, which was his way of conveying his own experience and understanding of the path and where it leads. He invited his listeners to imagine someone who is wandering in a forest and stumbles upon the ruins of an ancient, abandoned road. He follows it, and it leads him to the ruins of an ancient city with wonderful amenities and prospects. He returns to his own community and forcefully suggests to its authorities that they should restore this city, and the path leading to it. Some time later a thriving community is living in the restored city. Members of this community are bringing the fourfold task to bear on their life processes, which still feature the usual elements of dukkha – that is, of human life on planet Earth.

The Buddha never saw himself as a prophet with stunning cosmic revelations in his kitbag. He assumes that what he discovers, others would have already discovered before him long ago. Hence the ancient path and city just waiting to be rediscovered.

The new city dwellers are leading *dharmic* lives: they are alert witnesses to (and participants in) everyday conditionality. Stephen draws a cheeky contrast between St Augustine's terminally boring utopia, the City of God, full of standardised pure spirits whose feet never touch the ground, on the one hand; and on the other, the Buddha's City of Contingency, full of flourishing human beings dealing skilfully with the ups and downs of their grounded lives.

The path is not just an individual solution – it's a communal aspiration to live in *this* world in the most meaningful way possible.

Questions for study

1. To what extent do you agree with Stephen's decision to translate sammā as 'complete' rather than 'right'? Can you state the argument clearly and concisely?

2. What can you do to reduce the number of occasions when you are 'caught up in the habits, fixations, prejudices or biases of the mind'?

3. According to Stephen's use of the term, one who has 'entered the stream' has made the eightfold path their own. Do you consider yourself to have entered the stream in this respect? What are your priorities for cultivating the path?

4. How would you explain the difference between aligning your actions to an ethic, such as the dharma, on the one hand; and on the other, a moral code?

5. Stephen suggests that the ancient city in the parable 'symbolises a flourishing communal life based on the principle of conditionality as refracted through each facet of the fourfold task'. Can you see this kind of way of living taking root during your lifetime? What would have to happen in order for such an ideal to come to pass? Would you think it worthwhile to work towards it?

6. Stephen writes that 'in comparing the aim of his teaching to the rebuilding of an ancient city, the Buddha presents his goal as something entirely secular.' How does this contrast with your understanding of the 'goal' of the Buddhist tradition that you're most familiar with?

⌀ Session six:
Pasenadi, the king

Alternating more abstract with more concrete chapters in his book, Stephen now presents us, in his fourth chapter, with another important character from the Pali canon. This time around, the character in question is the Buddha's somewhat problematic friend, Pasenadi, king of Kosala, to whom the Buddha's own political community, Sakiya, pays tribute as a vassal state.

Political units in the Ganges region at this time (fifth century BCE) were small, numerous and inclined to make war against each other. There were two especially warlike monarchies (Kosala and Magadha), and five smaller oligarchical republics, of which Sakiya was one. The kings and chiefs in question were essentially warlords – often fickle and leading insecure lives, but (as in Pasenadi's case) also influenced by basic ideas about the duties and responsibilities of rulers.

All this complicates the friendship between the two protagonists. Pasenadi is a sincere convert to the dharma and obviously defers to the Buddha in spiritual and ethical matters. He has an inquiring bent and constantly engages the Buddha in conversation about questions that pique his curiosity or worry him.

But as a warlord and ruler in turbulent times, he's highly distracted, corrupted by wealth and power, and morally compromised by the dirty deeds he has to commit to keep it all together. We'll come to an example shortly.

For his part, the Buddha depends on his conflicted friend to support and protect his community, so he has to use all his 'people skills' to speak honestly but diplomatically. Not only that: the Buddha himself also grew up as a member of the warrior caste, the ruling elite, and so he understands the issues that Pasenadi faces.

Like his Greek contemporary, Socrates, the Buddha almost always taught through dialogue with others. Remarkably, the Pali canon records more conversations with Pasenadi than with anyone else. So let's have a look at some of the things they talked about, and how they sparked off each other's ideas when talking to others. Sometimes references to Pasenadi also enlivened dialogue with still others, as in the following example.

We don't rule over our body/minds

In a dialogue between the Buddha and Saccaka, a Jain teacher, the latter (in flat contradiction of the Buddha's teaching) preaches identification with the five bundles (*khandhas*) of experience that constitute a human being. He says: 'This body is my self, feelings are my self, [and so on with perceptions, inclinations, and consciousness].' Instead of failing Saccaka on the spot, the Buddha asks him if he believes in the unfettered prerogatives of the two reigning kings in the region – Pasenadi, and Ajātasattu of Magadha – to have people executed, fined or banished when necessary. Saccaka believes these prerogatives are legitimate, as the Buddha seems to as well.

But the Buddha is actually using kingship as a counterfactual. If each of the bundles was indeed 'my self', he says, then I would have a comparable power to rule over my bodily states, thoughts and emotions. In reality we have no such power – they arise dependent on conditions independent of our will. When we viscerally experience our powerlessness over them, we actually have a liberating experience of not-self. There is no core, regal *self* lurking in any of these bundles of experience, or in the sum of them, and we can stop clinging to them as if there were one.

The Buddha doesn't lay claim to omniscience

Then we come to Pasenadi himself in an odd little drama. The Buddha and Pasenadi are watching a procession of ascetics and wanderers as it passes by. The king makes elaborate homage to them, and then tells the Buddha that all these men are arahants, true saints. The Buddha's reply comes down to: *Yeah, right. How d'you know?* But he says it diplomatically, explaining that only a very good judge of character with a lot of experience of another person could tell if she or he were indeed an arahant.

Most conventional Buddhists would find this passage surprising. Isn't the Buddha supposed to be omniscient and able to get the measure of another person just by glancing at them? But here we have the no-magic-tricks Buddha disavowing any such supernatural insight, and affirming good old common sense instead.

At this point it seems that Pasenadi has anyway been playing a trick on everyone, and the Buddha has now effectively called him out. Pasenadi confesses that the men in question are his undercover agents sent out disguised as ascetics to spy on spiritual communities. His showy homage to them simply shores up their cover story. After this encounter he'll meet them in private, milk them of the information they've gathered, and then turn on some good old sensual pleasures for them.

Carelessness and care

Instead of exercising oracular powers, the Buddha exercised something more useful: the therapeutic skill of creating the space and the trust in which his interlocutor could articulate an insight for her- or himself. So we find Pasenadi announcing to the Buddha: 'Few are those people in the world who, when they obtain superior possessions, don't become intoxicated and careless, yield to greed for sensual pleasures, and mistreat other beings.'

It's unlikely that Pasenadi stumbles on this truth having just seen the film version of Scott Fitzgerald's novel *The Great Gatsby*. Rather, it's a painful moment of self-insight and justified self-accusation. And the Buddha doesn't rush in to contradict him. He simply replies: 'So it is, great king. So it is.'

This issue of *carelessness* – so well illustrated in Fitzgerald's *Gatsby* – segues into the central teaching around care itself. Is there a master virtue that secures all kinds of good? Pasenadi asks the Buddha on another occasion. Yes, the Buddha replies, it is **care** (*appamāda*).

Like some other key Pali words, *appamāda* is negative in form, and translates literally as non-carelessness. But like our word 'care', it has great depth and breadth to signify *a whole world of aware and ethical engagement*. Stephen here captures a very useful affinity to Martin Heidegger's discussion of *Sorge* (the German word for care) in his *Being and time*. Being fully human ('being-there' and 'being-in-the-world') is essentially driven by care, as both the Buddha and Heidegger affirm.

'Care is the sensibility that guides one's relationship with life as a whole,' Stephen comments. 'Care lies at the heart of the four tasks themselves, infusing and motivating each one of them. To genuinely care for the world means to embrace suffering, let go of one's selfish reactivity, behold ceasing of such reactivity, and cultivate an integrated way of life' (p.104). To care is to tread the path itself.

Thanks to a tragic quirk of the human condition, though, it's not all plain sailing. Both Christianity and Buddhism have produced eloquent witnesses to our almost intractable tendency to stuff up what we care about. St Paul writes: 'I don't understand what I do.

For what I want to do, I don't do; but what I hate to do I do … This I keep on doing.'

The great Buddhist poet Shantideva writes eight centuries later: 'Although wishing to be rid of misery, people run towards misery itself. Although wishing to have happiness, like an enemy they ignorantly destroy it.' In the Pali canon, Māra personifies this tragic flaw: carelessness – 'the banality of evil', as Hannah Arendt puts it. And Māra goes on stalking the Buddha, albeit to no effect, until the Buddha draws his last breath.

Love, joy and grief

Another big issue around care arises in an unexpected way. A man whose only son has died has become unhinged by the intensity of his grief, and seeks solace from the Buddha. He frankly tells the father that he has lost control of his mind in the face of a perfectly foreseeable predicament, for 'sorrow, lamentation, pain, grief and despair are born from those who are dear.' The father retorts, 'No, happiness and joy are born from those who are dear!'

The interchange gets back to Pasenadi, who tells his wife Mallikā about it. She just replies, the Buddha's right. But Pasenadi agrees with the father – with the conventional wisdom – and flies into a rage. When he's calmed down, Mallikā tries a different tack with him. How would you feel if one of your wives or children died or your kingdom was destroyed? She asks him. At that point Pasenadi comes around: 'How could sorrow, lamentation, pain, grief, and despair not arise in me?'

We know from other references to Mallikā that she's wise and tactful, and in this instance she's standing in for the Buddha, communicating something important in concrete, everyday terms, not in abstractions. She's pragmatic in the philosophical sense: a statement is true if it's useful, not if it's dogmatically 'right'. In fact, both statements about those who are dear to us are true, but not at the same time.

Here's Kahlil Gibran on this point: 'When you are sorrowful look again in your heart, and you shall see that in truth you are weeping for that which has been your delight.'

Healthy self-love gives birth to empathy

Mallikā once more plays this role as the Buddha's mouthpiece in the most popular of the teachings in this chapter. Pasenadi asks her if there's anyone more dear to her than herself – no doubt hoping she'd name him. But she says no, there's no-one else that answers that description. Pasenadi realises that the same is true for him, but it troubles him enough to report the exchange to the Buddha, who agrees that Mallikā is right: 'each person holds himself most dear; *hence one who loves himself should not harm others.*'

A pre-existing *upanishad* (Brahmanical teaching) affirmed the primacy of self-love, but drew a very different conclusion: it enjoins us to indulge it (narcissistically) as an intimation of our own divine immortality. For the Buddha, by contrast, self-love is the springboard into empathy. Other people foster the same self-love as we do; their hopes, joys and sorrows have the same weight and dignity as our own, and on this basis we can resonate with their experience, and *care* about them.

Modern philosophers call this sentiment *intersubjectivity* – an ethical stance that opposes the ubiquitous *instrumental rationality* that our socioeconomic system inculcates in us. According to the latter, other people are either useful to us, or getting in our way, and should be treated accordingly, with the addition of self-serving moralising according to taste. Such is the culture of today's neoliberalism.

Instrumental rationality sets up a subject-object relationship between self and other, whereby others are either a means or an obstacle to one's own egotistical ends. By contrast, intersubjectivity, exemplified by the dharma, sets up a two-way subject-subject relationships as the basis of an ethical life.

The Keynesian Buddha

The Buddha applies his ethic of care to financial affairs. Pasenadi tells him that a certain moneylender has died without heirs, and he (the king) has to see to it that the man's wealth finds its way safely into the royal coffers. The deceased has lived like pauper, and Pasenadi is amazed and delighted to discover that he has squirrelled away a vast fortune. Was not the deceased's lifestyle praiseworthy, then? he asks the Buddha. (If only he'd been able to read about the miserable Ebenezer Scrooge in Dickens's *A Christmas Carol!*)

The Buddha will have none of it, of course. He retorts: 'When an inferior man gains abundant wealth, he does not make himself, his family, his slaves, servants or employees happy... That wealth, not being used properly, goes to waste, not to utilisation' (p.107). Whereas a wise person uses his wealth by distributing it generously. Money should be in circulation, especially in the service of generosity.

The late-sixteenth/early-seventeenth century English polymath Francis Bacon, who could turn out aphorisms for all occasions as readily as the Buddha, once remarked that wealth was like muck – all the better for being well spread. Closer to our own time, the economic theorist John Maynard Keynes *proved* this to be the case.

Once again, the Buddha reveals his pragmatism, this time laced with crypto-Keynesianism.

Questions for study

1. Does Pasenadi remind you of anyone; another historical or fictional character perhaps? For example, to what extent does he sound like the legendary King Arthur?

2. Have you experienced not-self? If so, did you find it liberating? Try to be as specific as possible, drawing from your own experience in meditation and everyday life.

3. What experience have you had of being 'spied upon' by authority represented by snoopers like the fake ascetics in the story? When you found out about the snooping how did you feel, and how did you react or respond? What do you think about the way that the Buddha dealt with this situation?

4. What would the actions of a person guided by the master virtue of care look like? How might they differ from those of a person whose primary approach is compassion?

5. Right at this moment in time, do you feel more inclined towards the view 'Sorrow, lamentation, pain, grief and despair are born from those who are dear' or towards the view 'Happiness and joy are born from those who are dear'? Looking at these as two ends of a spectrum, how has your position varied over the past decade (or more), and what led to the shift?

6. Is there anyone more dear to you than yourself? Be honest. Examine any discomfort that might come from answering this question frankly.

7. If you had abundant wealth, how might you best use it? Does the Buddha's injunction to be generous have any impact on the way that you choose to deal with your wealth (financial, or otherwise)?

⌀ Session seven:
Letting go of truth

In his fifth chapter Stephen presents us with another more general teaching from the Pali canon. To my mind, this one in particular exemplifies the central point of Stephen's project of looking deeply into the Buddha's discourses without reference to the commentators' twists and turns that have obscured them since his death.

Suppose, for a moment, that we've acquired a very old building and want to refurbish it to render it once more usable in our own time, yet able to serve its original purpose. Our problem is that successive former owners have piled additional storeys onto it and added extensions, growing it like Topsy, such that the foundations have been covered over and the original design is no longer discernible.

But we have an intuition that the foundations and original design of the building might be far more appropriate to what we have in mind than the end result of all the bolt-on extensions and renovations that confront us.

So our own refurbishment has to start with a good deal of demolition of what's been added, in the course of which we uncover the original foundations. And just as we suspected, they're much more fit-for-purpose for recreating an edifice that satisfies today's requirements and sensibilities, and would blend in with its current surroundings. In fact, we're amazed at how brilliantly the original architect anticipated today's requirements. This analogy might be the best way to capture what Stephen is doing in his book, and particularly in this crucial chapter.

'Letting go' of truth

Like everyone else, Stephen tackles his task from a certain perspective. In his case that perspective is western post-metaphysical philosophy, which started in the late nineteenth century with Friedrich Nietzsche on the eastern side of the Atlantic, and the pragmatist philosophers on the western side.

'God is dead,' Nietzsche declared. He wasn't drafting God's death certificate, merely remarking that it'd been a while since western thinkers had referred to God as the ultimate source of everything, including human understanding. Nietzsche was much more interested in what this death meant for any idea of ultimate truth over and above what was evident in our own experience of the world. Ultimate truth had died with its source, he concluded.

The philosophers that Stephen names in passing in this chapter – Martin Heidegger, Gianni Vattimo, and the American pragmatists – proceed on this basis. They reject what's called *the correspondence theory of truth* – the idea that a statement or a theory can correspond with absolute reality, that is, some ultimate truth.

In popular parlance 'pragmatism' can edge into opportunism. But the philosophical pragmatists (John Dewey, William James and Richard Rorty are the important ones in this context) reject opportunism and actually have a strong ethical position: the driving motivation for any human inquiry must be human flourishing. They still have a use for some version of truth, but it doesn't mean ultimate truth – rather, the test of truth is whether it helps to create a better world, one more conducive to human flourishing.

The Buddha anticipated this stance in distinguishing between the first path factor of *sammā ditthi* (complete or 'right' view) and its opposite, *micchā ditthi* (inadequate or 'false' view). Complete view (or 'reality construct', if you like) inspires and focuses effective practice, whereas inadequate or 'false' view misleads and obstructs effective practice. Ultimate truth has nothing to do with it.

Dharmic truth

Through his own explorations of the Buddha's discourses, Stephen discloses a teacher who's on the same page as these latter-day thinkers. 'I don't say "this is true," which is what fools say to each other,' the Buddha declares on one occasion (p.115). Elsewhere he talks about truth – just like the pragmatists – as an ethical virtue. When we discussed the chapter on the Buddha's cousin Mahānāma, we found the Buddha bestowing on him the supreme accolade of being 'a true person'.

When the Buddha refers to himself with the Delphic expression, the *tathāgata* ('the one thus gone') he's referring to true personhood. The *tathāgata* exercises integrity, and doesn't pretend, dissemble, manipulate or betray.

As noted before, slightly old-fashioned English uses 'true' in two distinct senses. Ultimate truth is one usage – a hangover from Christianity; but the other usage refers to an ethical virtue that encompasses integrity, honesty, loyalty and transparency. So we talk about a true friend, or someone being true to their values (thus not being gutless or hypocritical); and we might ask a life partner who's just returned after an absence: 'Have you been true to me?'

The Buddha taught an ethical path of practice. Full stop. He left us with a how-to manual to guide us towards becoming 'true persons' – ethical agents in the process of realising our true human potential, that is, in the process of flourishing. The correspondence theory of truth in the form of metaphysical speculation was doing the rounds in his day and created endless distractions from practice, as he himself remarked on many occasions. He taught know-how, not capital-K Knowledge.

Yet every strand of ancestral Buddhism alive and well today touts a concept of ultimate truth in the form of the two-truths doctrine. According to it, truth comes in two packages: conventional truth (based on everyday experience) and ultimate truth (accessed by realised holy persons only). In spite of the ubiquity of this idea, it has no backing whatsoever in the Buddha's teaching. Certain central teachings, such as the *Sabbe sutta*, are flatly incompatible with it. So where does it come from?

Religious truth

Thereby hangs an interesting tale. The period during which the Pali canon was 'open' to new material (and to tweaking) lasted around four hundred years after the Buddha's death. It spanned an earlier period when the canon was a purely oral tradition, and a later period when it was committed to writing on (perishable) palm leaves.

During that time the Buddha's tradition came under the heavy influence of Brahmanism, an essentially theistic doctrine that posited the ultimate unity of all things in the godhead, Brahman. It legitimated a professional priesthood with supposed privileged access to ultimate truth about all this. The ultimate truth trumped conventional truth – the everyday experience of ordinary folk.

The canon was tweaked accordingly to make the dharma fit the template of an Indian religion. So metaphysical, ultimate truth insinuated itself into the dharma, and a theistic shadow was thereby cast over it.

These days, there's a whole body of literature dedicated to the death of God à la Nietzsche. One writer, Terry Eagleton, tells us that moving on from God's death hasn't been as easy as we thought, because people invented all sorts of surrogates and viceroys to replace him as a repository of ultimate realities. In *Culture and the death of God*, his list includes Reason, Nature, Geist, culture, art, the nation, the state, science, humanity, Being, Society, desire, the life force, and personal relations. All of them have acted from time to time as forms of displaced divinity. Jumping clear of these displaced divinities, along with their metaphysics and ultimate truths, is quite an athletic achievement!

In this context, Stephen makes his own point that western converts to Buddhism take readily to brahmanised versions of the dharma, conditioned as we are by the long shadow that the defunct Christian god still casts over our culture and mindset. A good example of this is the current popularity of mixing a dash of Advaita Vedanta in with western dharma practice and teaching.

Advaita Vedanta is an esoteric school of Hinduism which emphasises the importance of submitting to a guru under whose guidance the disciple ultimately penetrates the true divinity and non-duality of things. Dharma practice then becomes a mission to cultivate deep insight into the ultimate nature of reality, and thereby achieve final enlightenment, together with 'salvation' with the end of suffering, which is supposedly born of ignorance.

Restoring the Buddha's dharma

The Buddha introduced a practice (the fourfold task) and an eightfold path in which to frame it. It's an ethical path that informs all aspects of a practitioner's life. The practice and the path begin with a personal, intimate conversion (stream entry) – the result of first hearing the heartbeat of the dharma.

In Stephen's words, this stream entry leads us into 'a way of life in which one is true to one's potential, true to one's deepest intuitions, true to one's values, true to one's friends, and – as a Buddhist – true to the rationale (*thāna*) of the dharma... it has to do with leading a life of integrity, transparency, and honesty in everything one does' (p.149). One undertakes this practice 'independent of others,' not subservient to gurus and experts.

Referring to my opening image of refurbishing an ancient build-ing, the project begins by stripping away the later additions that have turned this ethical, engaged, immediately-available practice into a religion – one demanding adherence to a rhetoric of ultimate truth, and managed by a privileged priestly elite.

Questions for study

1. Imagine that Stephen's thesis – that the capital-T Truths in traditional Buddhism are later additions, and the Buddha's teachings were a pragmatic guide to human flourishing – was somehow verified beyond any reasonable doubt: would this be a problem for you? For anyone that you know? What difficulties might you or they face in coming to terms with this?

2. Imagine that Stephen's thesis was somehow shown to be false, beyond any reasonable doubt: would this be a problem for you? For anyone that you know? What difficulties might you or they face in coming to terms with this?

3. Do you accept or reject the correspondence theory of truth? Are your actions consistent with your viewpoint on the validity of the correspondence theory of truth?

4. A school textbook on comparative religion asks a question: 'What do Buddhists believe?' Why do you think the textbook's author included a question like this, and how do you think they intended it to be answered?

5. Imagine that in the future an equivalent textbook makes the assertion 'Buddhists like Stephen Batchelor say that the Buddha taught know-how, not Knowledge with a capital K.' How would you unpack this statement in such a way that a 12-year-old could make sense of it?

6. Do you recognise from your own experience of life any of the forms of displaced divinity identified by Terry Eagleton? What use did the form have, as a surrogate source of ultimate truths? How obvious was it that these posited ultimate truths may have eventually been a distraction from living in a more ethical way?

7. Have you had any experience, positive or negative, in dealing with self-proclaimed gatekeepers of ultimate truth? Have you yourself ever found yourself taking on this authority?

Ⓢ Session eight:
Sunakkhatta: the traitor

As noted in earlier sessions, Stephen's book plunges into the Pali canon in an original way, alternating more abstract chapters with accounts of some of the Buddha's associates which we can glean from the discourses that present them. Chapter six of *After Buddhism* deals with a not-so-illustrious character called Sunakkhatta, who ended up becoming disillusioned with the Buddha, quitting the ranks of his mendicant followers, and denouncing him. The chapter has three main focuses:

- Ⓢ the shifting and confusing projections onto the Buddha from his own time to ours;
- Ⓢ the confusions (personified by Sunakkhatta) that arise when we allow our pursuit of 'religious experiences' to deflect our spiritual practice; and
- Ⓢ the dharmic 'tragic vision' that the Buddha's own life displays at this point.

Projections onto the Buddha
In the real heat-and-dust world of the Ganges region in the fifth century BCE that the Buddha inhabited, Brahmanism (early Hinduism) hadn't yet achieved its hegemony, and sometimes fierce competition reigned between teachers and gurus in what was an

open spiritual market.

One of the Buddha's contemporary rivals, for instance, was Mahāvīra, founder of Jainism, which shares some common ground with the Buddhadharma and still has adherents in India today, especially in professional and business circles.

The usual way to succeed in this competitive market was to establish charismatic authority in one or both of two ways: holding out the promise of euphoric 'religious experiences' (or 'peak experiences' in our modern term) laced with esoteric truth-claims about the cosmos and showy miracles; or exceeding in austerities (self-torment, self-punishment).

The Brahmans and many other teachers offered both, while Mahāvīra and his followers excelled in austerities. The Buddha's problem was that he eschewed both these sorts of commodities, which had little relevance to spiritual practice as he understood it. In the resulting sectarianism, Mahāvīra's followers saw the Buddha as 'addicted to luxury' because he didn't practise or advocate extreme austerities.

In the previous session, we noted how the period during which the contents of the Pali canon were still up for grabs lasted for around 400 years after the Buddha's death. During that time Brahmanism did consolidate its hegemony, and apocryphal material from that source found its way into the discourses as the Pali canon recorded them.

As Stephen puts it, after the Buddha's death, 'his community was fatally weakened by its gradual, tacit assent to the norms and values of Brahmanic culture' (p.154). And so remains in many iterations of actually-existing Buddhism today, which is why Stephen has called his book *After Buddhism*: it's what we can restore after we strip out the Brahmanic accretions in conventional Buddhism.

Some of these accretions packaged the Buddha in magical ways to pump up his charismatic authority. Stephen mentions the Brahmanic thirty-two marks of a great being that the Buddha posthumously acquired, including the Bodhi protrusion sticking up out of the crown of his head, chariot wheels stencilled onto the soles of his feet, a tongue capable of licking his ears and forehead, etc. You can compare this with the stigmata and haloes that adorn holy persons in traditional Christian pictures.

All of this conveyed the idea that the Buddha was no mere mortal: he'd descended from another realm entirely. Among other things, Stephen is restoring the Buddha ('Gotama', or 'Mr Gotama' as many contemporaries addressed him) to his actual human form. He taught about the human condition, something he was immersed in himself.

Sunakkhatta's problem

Our friend Sunakkhatta hankered after the conventional promises that drew high prices in the religious marketplace: ecstatic experiences, miracles, and esoteric cosmic revelations. As Stephen describes him, he's 'an idealist who yearned for mystical experiences and metaphysical certainties' (p.155). And that's precisely what he doesn't get from the Buddha.

So he tells the powerful Vesālī assembly that Gotama 'does not have any superhuman states, any distinction in knowledge and vision worthy of the noble ones. [He] teaches a dharma hammered out by reasoning, following his own line of enquiry as it occurs to him, and when he teaches the dharma to anyone, it leads when he practises it to the complete end of suffering.'

To our ears, this denunciation sounds more like a promo, and that's how the Buddha heard it, too. 'Thinking to discredit me,' he says, '[Sunakkhatta] actually praises me; for it is praise of me to say: "when he teaches the dharma to anyone, it leads when he practises it to the complete end of suffering".' (p.151).

From ending suffering to ending reactivity

For Sunakkhatta, the complete end of suffering doesn't seem to appeal at all – it's too banal, presumably. He's looking for something more grandiose, including celestial music in his meditative absorptions. In previous sessions we've seen that, when we unpack it, this banal goal is both bigger and smaller than it sounds. In his key references to the goal of practice, the Buddha refers to nirvana, which means the complete end of reactivity.

In the first discourse, the Buddha unpacked *dukkha*, and every item in it necessarily inheres in the human condition. Nirvana isn't the end of the human condition, it's the end of the *reactivity* we bring to the difficult aspects of every human life that stops us flourishing as only a human being can.

As the saying goes: you can't stop the waves, but you can learn to surf. This requires of us *imperturbability (āneñja)* – more commonly known today as resilience. It's the underpinning of a steady focus, a probing awareness, and sustained care around our practice. Earlier in their association, the Buddha delivered a teaching to Sunakkhatta on this subject, but it wasn't what the latter was looking for.

The dharma and tragic vision

There's a convergence between the Buddha's teaching and our western tradition – going back to the Greeks – of tragic vision. Both see us at the mercy of forces and processes that can crash down on us at any time, and will ultimately destroy us. These are not 'problems' to be solved so we can get back to what we thought we were somehow guaranteed – a secure and fortunate life of our own choosing. Rather, these are conditions are to be endured with all our human courage, wisdom and dignity, so that we can say yes to life in all circumstances.

The Buddha's situation at the time of Sunakkhatta's betrayal is indeed tragic. He's 80 years old, living out his final months in pain and decrepitude, with his long-term patrons and places of refuge no longer available to him. His closest friends (Sāriputta and Moggallāna) have recently died, and the whole region is about to plunge into war and genocide. His world is falling apart. And yet this is when the Buddha achieves intense dignity and rounds out his teaching, day after day on his final journey, as related in the long *Parinibbāna sutta*.

Barry Hill interviews the Dalai Lama in an article that is nicely entitled, 'On the edge of a cliff.' It appears in the September 2015 issue of *The Monthly*. It's astonishing to see the similarity between the Dalai Lama's predicament and the one in which we find the Buddha in Stephen's chapter. The Dalai Lama is also 80 years old, an exile, recent renunciant of all his temporal powers, and spiritual leader of a poor outcast people with no discernible hope of ever reclaiming their homeland. Yet he's one of the most famous individuals in the world and almost certainly the most respected, given that his influence reaches well beyond the Buddhist world.

It's in tragic circumstances that the human spirit burns brightest. Shakespeare's arguably greatest tragedy is *King Lear*. When the protagonist reaches rock bottom on the heath, in a storm and with no protection, he blurts out his (self-)description of the human being as 'a poor bare, forked animal' (act 3 scene 4). And he begins to attain a majesty he never dreamed existed while he was a foolish and arrogant monarch.

Questions for study

1. Accusing the Buddha of being 'addicted to luxury' probably sounds like an exaggeration for comic effect. Can you recall a time when, in all seriousness, you made an equally preposterous accusation about someone? What do you think might have been your motivations at the time, and was there anything specific that made you later realise that you were overreaching?

2. How do you feel about the idea of stripping out the Brahmanical accretions that are part of conventional Buddhism? What do you think ought to be done with those elements which have been stripped out? How much are your thoughts on this influenced by your general attitude towards tradition in general?

3. Stephen describes Sunakhatta as 'an idealist who yearned for mystical experiences and metaphysical certainties'. The word 'idealist' could mean a person who represents things as they might or should be rather than as they are, or it could be used in the philosophical sense to mean someone who asserts that reality as humans can know it is immaterial. Which type of idealist do you think best matches the sense in which Stephen uses it here?

4. What do you understand to be the difference between 'the dharma leading to the complete end of suffering' and 'the dharma leading to the complete end of reactivity'? Is either of these ends achievable, or are they aspirational? What might it be like if one who had ended suffering met one who had ended reactivity, and what might they say to one another?

5. In what sense is the Buddha's situation at the time of Sunakhatta's betrayal tragic? Do you find the Buddha's story, or that of the Dalai Lama cathartic? What meaning do you find in the story of the Buddha's betrayal by Sunakhatta?

∅ Session nine:
On experience

As noted in earlier sessions, in *After Buddhism* Stephen alternates chapters about actual individuals who practised under the Buddha's own guidance with chapters on more abstract topics. Chapter seven, on experience, clearly belongs to the latter category.

This is a somewhat challenging chapter, but as usual, the difficulty lies not so much in the new ideas as in getting rid of the old ones. This chapter delves into distinctions that seem at first sight to be quite fiddly, but turn out to resolve extraordinarily important confusions about the thrust of the dharma and its practice. Here Stephen melds a very close reading of relevant discourses with his knowledge of phenomenology, which sometimes presents the distinctions he wants to make more sharply.

The background to all this is Stephen's sense that, at key points, conventional Buddhism (and the orthodox Theravāda in particular) has misread the early teachings and *misrepresented them as metaphysics rather than as an ethics*. This has reframed the dharma as a religion like any other, offering revelations about the way things supposedly really are behind their 'mere' appearances.

In contrast, the Buddha refuses to drive a wedge between how we experience things and the way they supposedly really are. Phenomenology makes exactly the same point.

The centrality of experience

The Buddha's key working terms all spring from his placing human experience centre stage. Dharma practice is about coming to terms with human experience itself – including *experientially* overcoming habitual ways of perceiving things, by experiencing them with far greater attention and commitment.

So the Buddha treats as synonymous terms that – in everyday parlance – we would see as unrelated. For instance, 'everything' (*sabbe*) equates with the practitioner's domain (*visaya*), with the world (*loka*) and with *dukkha* (the tragic dimension of human life). Why is this? Because they all need to be understood as encompassed by human experience, not as cosmic concepts detached from how we experience them. *'The world' is what is happening and being experienced right now.*

We can compare these terms with a key one in phenomenology: *life-world*. If we really want to understand our experience, we don't start by seeing ourself as one organism among trillions on planet Earth. Rather, we examine the world that we ourselves touch, live and breathe – our home, our culture, our family, relationships, friendships, work community, personal projects, and so on.

We can only live as ourselves in constant interaction with our life-worlds. This interaction constitutes us. We wouldn't be who we are without it. And the life-world in question is in constant flux and disruption. To understand it and ourselves we have to embrace this flux and disruption as it manifests in our own experience. This is the first of the four dharmic tasks Stephen retrieved in his chapter three (our session 4): *embrace dukkha* – the human condition.

As we pay attention to our experience – primarily in the practice of insight meditation – we're developing a first-person consciousness of our experience. We ourselves are inseparable from the experience we're focusing in on. In other words, we have to break with the usual mindset that splits us off from our experience, resulting in a knowing subject confronting known objects. Each of us is *always already* fully engaged in our experience – we can't pretend to be standing somewhere else looking in.

The Buddha wasn't interested in revelations, but rather in an effective ethical practice whereby we can experience for ourselves that we can leave behind unhelpful patterns of habitual reactions, and make other choices based on a growing understanding of our life experience. Or, as Stephen puts it, the dharma comprises *a task-based ethics, not a truth-based metaphysics*.

Learning to pay sufficient attention to our experience to achieve this understanding and freedom, and to put our new choices into practice, constitutes a deeply transformative way of life.

The five bundles

Everything the Buddha taught in aid of this project arose from his own pragmatic standpoint. So the key teaching of the five bundles (*khandhas*) represents his suggestion for how we can tease out different elements of our experience which, at first blush, seems to be unitary and seamless.

So he's *not* revealing some eternal truth that our experience consists of these five bundles: our physicality, our hedonics, our perceptions, inclinations, and consciousness. Rather, he's saying that if we parse these elements out of our at-first undifferentiated experience, we'll see our patterns more clearly.

Why is this approach based on the five bundles so helpful? Well, mainly because they give us a vantage point on where our human shoes tend to pinch – where *dukkha* arises, and where our habitual reactivity begins.

Nāmarūpa

Another entry point for penetrating first-person human experience is the concept of *nāmarūpa*, which the Buddha stole from the Brahmanic tradition and radically repurposed. We encounter it most often in the teaching of the *nidānas*, or links in the chain of causation. *Nāmarūpa* literally means 'nameform', but conventional Buddhism mischievously inserts an 'and' in the middle, to make 'name-and-form', and so throws us back into the unhelpful subject/object, mind/body distinctions we need to avoid.

As against that, nameform (as the Buddha deploys it) is virtually synonymous with the phenomenologist Martin Heidegger's key expressions 'being-there' (*Dasein*) and 'being-in-the-world' (*In-der-Welt-sein*). The components of nāma are touch, feeling, perception, intention and attention. Rūpa consists in the four great elements of earth, water, fire, air and the forms derived from them. These are the Buddha's terms for a human person, but ones inseparable from her life-world and her life-process. We are not already fully-formed individuals who experience things and decide to do things – rather, our engagement in life, which is *always already* on foot, constitutes who we are.

In dharmic terms, to be a human person – a nameform – is to be *always already* in touch with the world. In the Buddha's teaching this being-in-touch determines consciousness. But consciousness also conditions our being-in-touch. There can then be no pure, pristine, unconditioned consciousness – only consciousness born of living in the thick of it. A human person isn't a static, circumscribed entity, but a hub of complex living processes *which are always already on foot*, and forever changing.

It's *this* kind of conscious we need to reach for in meditation and in everyday life. We do so by cultivating what the Buddha called 'embodied attention' (*yoniso manasikāra*: literally, 'attention from the womb'). We're embodied beings in endless flux, so this is the true basis of our attention. From here we can begin to discern how our habitual perceptions deceive and mislead us, thus keeping us stuck. 'Embodied attention' – not a bad synonym for skilful insight meditation – subverts these habitual perceptions, and so releases our creativity.

Not-self and no-self

The mistake of translating nāmarūpa as mind-*and*-body is compounded by mistranslating *anattā* as no-self instead of not-self. 'No-self' would amount to a metaphysical assertion ('There is no self!') the likes of which the Buddha avoided like the plague. But *not*-self, on the other hand, is simply a facet of our experience that we discern when we pay close attention to it.

For reasons we've gone into in previous sessions, the Buddha assumes that selves exist and function – they're just not 'findable'. Hence Nāgājuna's riddle:

Were mind and matter me,
I would come and go like them.
If I were something else,
They would say nothing about me (p.178).

We mentioned earlier that the Buddha pinched the term *nāmarūpa* from the Brahmanic tradition, in which it referred to each person's particularity (or identity, we might say). The aim of spiritual practice in that tradition was (and remains in Hinduism) the ultimate dissolution of that particularity into the one all-encompassing, transpersonal godhead. That tradition expresses this idea in the metaphor of all the different rivers flowing into the one great ocean, thus losing their name, particularity or identity.

Unsurprisingly, the Buddha also stole and repurposed the metaphor as well. Now the great ocean represents the dharma and the community of its practitioners, which dissolve the aspects of the practitioners' former identities that obstruct and imprison them – caste or class in the first instance, but by implication any ascribed status-markers, such as gender – thus setting them free to become self-creating and freely-associating equal individuals.

For the Buddha, as for the Christian Bible, *it's the truth that sets us free.* But in the Buddha's case, that truth is purely experiential, and won through close embodied attention to our ever-changing process of being-in-the-world. That sounds like a pretty good manifesto for secular insight meditators!

Questions for study

1. In what way might the early teaching have been misrepresented as a metaphysics rather than an ethics? What do you think about orthodox Buddhism treating the dharma as a belief system?

2. Have you come to terms with the notion that dharma practice is about coming to terms with human experience itself? Or do you hold onto the idea that dharma practice is about transcending human experience?

3. How much aversion do you feel towards the thought of examining our individual life-worlds in order to come to terms with human experience? Does it feel solipsistic, and how do you feel about that?

4. Thinking about the way that you pay attention to your own experience, what does your first-person consciousness feel like? Is it completely subjective, completely objective, or somewhere in between? Or something else entirely? Have you ever tried to stand outside of your experience in order to examine it?

5. How compatible do you think the traditional rule-based morality (derived from a truth-based metaphysics) is with the task-based ethics promoted by Stephen? How possible is it to make a clear distinction between the two?

6. Can you explain how, from a phenomenological perspective, there can be no pure, pristine, unconditioned consciousness? What is the appeal of this ideal of a pure unconditioned consciousness? Why might it be a dead end in dharmic terms?

7. How accurate do you think the term 'embodied attention' is as a synonym for skilful insight meditation?

8. Using the metaphors of rivers flowing into the ocean, contrast the Brahmanic and dharmic ideals of spiritual practice. Suggest an alternative metaphor to help explain the difference between these two approaches.

9. What would you do with your freedom if you dissolved the identities that obstruct and imprison you?

✆ Session ten:
Jīvaka the doctor

Having worked through another abstract chapter of *After Buddhism* we're now due, in chapter eight, for one on an actual individual who practised under the Buddha's own guidance. This time it's the royal physician Jīvaka.

Jīvaka was one of the twenty-one adherents (laypeople) whom the Buddha recalled by name as having fully realised their dharma practice. As he put it: 'Possessing six qualities, the householder Jīvaka has found fulfilment in [the Buddha], has become a seer of the deathless, and goes about having beheld the deathless. What six? Lucid confidence in the Buddha, lucid confidence in the dharma, lucid confidence in the sangha, noble virtue, noble understanding, and noble liberation' (p.229).

He'd also been the Buddha's friend and physician during the late years, after they met when the Buddha was around 72 years old. But this connection doesn't exhaust Jīvaka's interest for us. His life story provides us with a valuable glimpse into the social and cultural world in which the Buddha himself lived – one that left formative traces on the first draft of the dharma that he produced. That might be a good place to start.

The bastard son
In various patriarchal cultures and eras, the illegitimate sons of

womanising grandees (such as kings) have classically played disruptive roles, because they're born to privilege and power but without settled expectations about their status in adult life. (Think: Edmund, bastard son of Gloucester in *King Lear*, and Goetz, the protagonist in Jean-Paul Sartre's long, intense play, *Lucifer and the lord*.)

King Bimbisāra of Magadha – the Buddha's fervent devotee and protector over many years – seems to have been otherwise oversexed, and fathered in particular two illegitimate sons by different mistresses: Abhaya and Jīvaka, as well as a legitimate son and heir, Ajātasattu. The grim Shakespeare-worthy family tragedy duly unfolded, but the usual roles were reversed: the bastard sons led meritorious lives, while the legitimate heir ended up overthrowing the king, imprisoning him, deliberately starving him to death, and usurping his throne.

Long before that, however, the two young illegitimate half-brothers each decided to learn a trade and make an honest living. Jīvaka chose to learn medicine from the renowned physician Atraya, who taught at the university in Taxilā (near today's Rawalpindi, Pakistan), the capital of Gandhāra, which would have involved him in what was an arduous 1,200 km hike through inhospitable regions, and seven years of dire poverty while he learned the art of healing.

But what a formative experience it must have been! Taxilā was a cosmopolitan city in touch with the civilisations of Persia, Greece, Egypt and Arabia. The university would have demanded that Jīvaka learn a lot more than medical skills – consisting of herbalism, diagnostics and surgery. Doctors at the time did not confine themselves to strictly physiological problems, but functioned as sages, philosophers and existential consultants.

Indeed, these roles overlapped, which is how Jīvaka and the Buddha found such essential common ground. There was no mind/body split back then, and neither of them had any use for dogmatism, metaphysics, or simplistic solutions. The Buddha frequently resorted to medical metaphors and analogies in his teaching, and was (and is) commonly referred to as the great physician of humankind. Though no actual doctor himself, he clearly knew a thing or two about the practice of medicine.

What we might recognise today as the strictly medical aspects of young Jīvaka's education were grounded and grounding. After seven years, Atraya ordered him to take a spade and a sack, search all the countryside around Taxilā to a radius of 15 km, and bring back any plant he found to have no medical use. Jīvaka returned from this errand with an empty sack, for which he received top marks.

Jīvaka proved himself an effective healer, and began to reap the material rewards of his skills back in his home town. He soon had his own clinic (which seems to have also housed in-patients, eventually including the Buddha himself when they met), and he became the physician at Bimbisāra's court after curing the king in short order of an embarrassing anal fistula.

When the Buddha and Jīvaka finally met, they did so as equals. For instance, the good doctor had no compunction in telling the teacher to stop his mendicants eating so much rich food for their health's sake, and to wear proper clothes instead of rags found around charnel grounds; and the Buddha seems to have acted on all such recommendations without demur.

Dharmic medicine

But the big story in this friendship turned on the convergence be-tween dharma and medicine as it was then practised. Stephen opens this chapter (at p.206) with a well-known teaching of the Buddha:

Suppose a man needing a snake, wandering in search of a snake, saw a large snake and grasped its coils or its tail. It would turn back on him and bite his hand or arm or one of his limbs, and because of that he would come to death or deadly suffering. Why? Because of his wrong grasp of the snake. So too, here some misguided people learn the dharma but having learned the dharma, *they do not examine the meaning of the teachings with intelligence, they do not arrive at a reasoned understanding of them.* Instead, they learn the dharma only for the sake of criticising others and winning in debates, and they do not experience the good for the sake of which they learned the dharma. These teachings, being wrongly grasped by them, conduce to their harm and suffering for a long time (p.206).

Of course someone who understood snakes wouldn't grasp one in the manner described, but would grab it just behind the head, so stopping it from striking back. The obvious message from this teaching is that the dharma – like so many tools we use and rely on today (cars, chainsaws, etc.) – is dangerous if not handled skilfully. It contains toxins that need to be handled and applied with skill and care. Those who use the dharma as a way of inflating their self-importance, and putting others down, risk the fate of the clumsy snake-handler in the parable.

But there's more to this story than meets the eye. Who on earth would 'need' a venomous snake, seek it, and wander in search of it? A physician like Jīvaka would. Snake venom in small amounts was the active ingredient in remedies for a number maladies, such as arthritis. (Recent research has found that snake venom in tiny quantities cures arthritis in rats.) So catching snakes, milking them of their venom, and measuring and mixing it with other ingredients to meet the needs of each individual patient, constituted normal clinical practice.

Devadatta: the clumsy dharma-handler

One who used the dharma unskilfully, and suffered the consequences, was the Buddha's cousin, Devadatta. As Ajātasatthu was making his move against his father, Devadatta – in league with the patricidal prince – made his move against the Buddha, seeking to displace him as the head of his movement.

Devadatta envied the love and respect that came his cousin's way, and he also turned the dharma into an ascetic dogma – thus ignoring the Buddha's condemnation of asceticism as a 'dead end' in his first teaching. It's a nice reminder – as if we needed one in the age of the Islamic State – that fundamentalism often arises to cloak a grab for power. Devadatta's own power-grab failed, but it split the sangha – a grave offence in the dharmic tradition – and thus branded him a schismatic.

Devadatta's campaign against the Buddha centred on vegetarianism, which he wanted to make an absolute rule. The Buddha vetoed him: as far as possible one should avoid killing and hurting living beings, but a mendicant has to live in the real world and eat whatever people choose to give her or him. The practitioner should engage with ordinary people, not stand aloof from them and judge them from some self-proclaimed high moral ground.

The Buddha's discourse *To Jīvaka*, which records these two friends' most significant conversation, held in the physician's clinic, turns on this very point. Is the rumour true, Jīvaka wants to know, that the Buddha 'knowingly eats meat prepared for him from animals killed for his sake?'

The Buddha's reply demonstrates his situational ethics. The dharma embodies the fundamental *ethic* of non-harming, but no ethical principle is well-served by blind obedience to *rules*. Ethically significant situations have to be understood in all their complexity, and the ethicist must exercise a judgement on what is the best course of action in the particular circumstances, and not follow the moralist into knee-jerkingly applying a rule no matter what.

One can well understand how this reply resonates with the physician's pragmatic approach to his own work. A good therapy is one that works, not one that conforms with the Vedas, or other expression of Absolute Truth, but doesn't work. He can never fall back on preconceived answers. At this point, Jīvaka solemnly commits to the dharma: 'Henceforth, please consider me an adherent who has gone for refuge for life.'

Nursing the sick and the first task

There's a yet more fundamental facet to the convergence of dharma and clinical practice in immediate responses to situations. Stephen raises it by recalling the account in the Vinaya of the Buddha and Ānanda arriving at a community of his mendicants, and coming across one of them lying alone in his own excrement, helpless and untended, presumably stricken with dysentery. The Buddha is clearly aghast at the other mendicants' neglect. He and Ānanda immediately respond to the sick man's plight by washing him, lifting him up, and putting him to bed. There's nothing metaphorical about this scene – no Great Physician parading his compassion. This is real-deal, jump-to-it nurse's-aid stuff.

Then the Buddha calls the community together and demands an explanation for the sick man's neglect. The reply is a chilling example of instrumental rationality – so alive and well in our time and place: 'This brother is of no use to us in his condition, so we don't bother looking after him.'

The Buddha's correction of this attitude is brief and to the point. He ends by saying: 'Whoever would tend to me should tend to the sick.' So he identifies himself with the sick; and those who care about him – for what he stands for – should care for the sick.

This is more than compassion in action: it's a powerful tackling of the first great task: embracing dukkha in the form of birth, sickness, ageing and death. Working in a labour ward, a clinic, an aged-care home or a hospice reveals the dharma to us as effectively as the Buddha himself. Every predicament in these places demands our immediate and creative response, not pat answers.

It sure worked for Jīvaka!

Questions for study

1. The Buddha used the phrase 'a seer of the deathless' to describe Jīvaka. What do you understand this phrase to mean, in this context?

2. In the Gospel of Mark, there is a passage where Jesus likens himself to a great physician:

> 'But when some of the Jewish religious leaders saw him eating with these men of ill repute, they said to his disciples, "How can he stand it, to eat with such scum?" When Jesus heard what they were saying, he told them, "Sick people need the doctor, not healthy ones! I haven't come to tell good people to repent, but the bad ones".' (Mark 2:16-17)

How does your understanding of Jesus the great physician compare with Gotama the great physician?

3. Adapt the passage about the snake so that it uses a more contemporary metaphor that would be better understood in your specific place and time. Once you have updated this parable, is there more to your new story than meets the eye? How does the different metaphor help you to understand the consequences of mishandling the dharma?

4. What 'moral high ground' do you stand on? Can you see what absolute rule that hill is built upon? What is the opposite of that absolute rule? Can you see how navigating a middle way between these two absolutes would be preferable, ethically speaking?

5. Can you think of any specific examples of an ethical principle that is not well-served by blind obedience to rules? Can you think of a specific example where an ethical principle is well-served by blind obedience to rules? How are rules limited by the language that we use to express them?

6. Considering the principle of pragmatism in the practice of medicine, find out about a specific advance in medical history that had better outcomes for the patient, but was resisted at the time. What were the reasons for the resistance, as you understand them? Can these reasons be traced back to a dogma, an absolute assumption, a tradition that would not respond to changes in conditions?

7. One final comparison with the Christian gospels: In the parable relating to the 'Final Judgement' (Matthew 25) the king who sits in judgement tells the righteous that, amongst other things that they did for him, they cared for him when he was sick. The righteous want to know when they ever saw the king sick and he replies: 'I tell you the truth, when you did it to one of the least of these my brothers and sisters, you were doing it to me!' How does this story from Jesus, as you understand it, compare with the Buddha's confrontation with the monastic community who had left the sick man alone, helpless and lying in his own excrement? Are these two stories moral stories?

∅ Session eleven:
The everyday sublime

In this session we're tackling one of *After Buddhism*'s general chapters, chapter nine. It concerns the thrust of the most important meditative practice that the Buddha taught: insight meditation – *satipatthāna* in Pali. Today in the west it's the main business of the conventional Buddhist vipassanā movements on the one hand, and the more secular insight meditation movements on the other. (Some of Sydney's insight sanghas spent a couple of years working their way through the Buddha's central teaching on this practice, the *Satipatthāna sutta*, before tackling *After Buddhism*.) Naturally, Stephen refers to it in this chapter, under the title *The grounding of mindfulness*, as he translates the title of this pivotal teaching. In more conventional circles it's called *The four foundations of mindfulness*.

This chapter of *After Buddhism* is very rich. Its contents go to the heart of dharma practice in the west. Rather than rush through them, we'll hold over discussion of its latter parts to the next session. In the present one we'll go as far as the end of section 4 on p.242.

Meditation: from technical skill to existential awareness

The chapter opens with an especially powerful paragraph:

Meditation originates and culminates in the everyday sublime. I have little interest in achieving states of sustained concentration in which the sensory richness of experience is replaced by pure introspective rapture. I have no interest in reciting mantras, visualising Buddhas or mandalas, gaining out-of-body experiences, reading other people's thoughts, practicing lucid dreaming, or channeling psychic energies through chakras, let alone letting my consciousness be absorbed in the transcendent perfection of the Unconditioned. Meditation is about embracing what is happening to this organism as it touches its environment in this moment. I do not reject the experience of the mystical. I only reject the view that the mystical is concealed behind what is merely apparent, that it is anything other than what is occurring in time and space right now. ***The mystical does not transcend the world but saturates it.*** 'The mystical is not how the world is,' noted Ludwig Wittgenstein in 1921, 'but that it is' (p.231).

There's a lot going on in this paragraph, so let's do a spot of unpacking. The term 'the sublime' here refers to experience that goes beyond words and other forms of representation – as the then 18-year-old Edmund Burke developed the notion in his first book, *The sublime and the beautiful* (1757), and as the Romantic poets later used the term. The sublime may inspire either awe or terror in us, or both. Because sublime experience can't be tamed and reduced to conventional words and pictures, it's often labelled as 'mystical'.

So how can such experiences attract the adjective 'everyday'? Almost certainly Stephen borrows this term from the foremost phenomenological thinker and a major influence on his own work, Martin Heidegger. Heidegger wanted to get to the bottom of the actual experience of being human as such – not in dramatic moments, but in our *average everydayness*, he writes, over and over.

What is being human *essentially* about? So far, the whole western philosophical tradition had avoided this question, he reckoned. The thing is: we spend our every moment embroiled in flux and uncertainty, with the only real certainty being death at the end.

Between the words 'sublime' and 'everyday' a creative tension reigns. The astronaut Michael Massimino has written a short memoir, 'A view of the earth', about the time he and a colleague are sent up in the shuttle *Atlantis* to replace a vital piece of electronic gear in the Hubble space telescope as it orbits the earth at an altitude of 600 km, and at around 30,000 km/h. (At that speed each lap around the earth takes just 90 minutes.) He and his colleague have trained together for years down on earth to carry out this sort of repair. No-one knows how to do this job like they do.

But unfortunately the gadget in question could only be accessed from outside the telescope, so the job requires him to take a spacewalk, somehow managing to cling onto the outer skin of the Hubble which 'has no good handrails', he notes laconically. He keeps his terror at bay by concentrating on the technicalities of the task. He's just a skilled tradesman doing a job, and that's his authorial voice as he tells his story. But then he strikes a hitch getting the access panel off, and Ground Control tell him to just stay put while they work out a solution. So there he is, hanging out (literally!) in outer space while he waits.

He feels a deep loneliness, he writes (pp.132–3). 'And it wasn't just a "Saturday afternoon with a book" alone ... everything I knew and loved and that made me feel comfortable was far away. And then it started to get dark and cold ... when you enter the darkness, it is not just darkness. It's the darkest black I have ever experienced ... It gets cold, and I could feel that coldness, and I could sense the darkness coming, and it just added to my loneliness.'

He looks down at the earth. 'And that moment changed my relationship with Earth. Because for me the Earth had always been a kind of safe haven ... where I could go to work or be in my home or take my kids to school. But I realised it really wasn't that. It really is its own spaceship. And I had always been a space traveler. All of us here today ... we're on the spaceship Earth, amongst all the chaos of the universe, whipping around the sun and the Milky Way galaxy' (pp.136–7).

A few days later he's back home, mission accomplished, the usual routines re-established. But nothing is ever the same for him again. In the dharmic terms we've explored earlier in this study series, he has loved, delighted, and revelled in his habitual place (*ālaya*). But through this sublime experience he's got a sense of something else entirely: the groundless ground (*taṇhā*) that is our true home, underneath the habituated ways we have of turning away from it. From the perspective of this ground, the core vision of the dharma, everyday life is indeed sublime – excessively rich, and so very precarious.

Here we come to the vital point of insight meditation, and of its core element: *sati* – recollection-and-mindfulness. 'Recollection' in a double sense: awareness of the flow of cause and effect in which the present experience is arising, and recollection of the core vision of the dharma. This is what receiving the present experience on its own terms ('mindfulness') is all about. It's the true chronicle of this groundless ground.

Thus, to get back to the last part of Stephen's opening paragraph, we shouldn't seek the sacred in a transcendent realm beyond ourselves or our world, but rather let it reveal itself when we quieten, relax our minds, and open our senses to what is happening right here and now. In meditation practice and in daily life. The mystical is not elsewhere, but here. It's what's happening right here and now. 'The mystical does not transcend the world but saturates it,' Stephen writes. The process starts with awareness of the body, and mindfulness of breathing is the conventional way into it. And we don't leave it behind as we attend to the other three focuses of awareness – feeling tones, emotions, and cognitive phenomena.

The ground of dharma

We saw earlier that the dharmic vision (*'this ground'*) rests on two pillars: *contingency* (aka 'conditionality', 'dependent arising' or 'cause-and-effect'); and *nirvana* (momentary complete absence of reactivity). But this ground is *duddaso*, difficult to see; and *duranubodha* (difficult to awaken to). The prefix *du* means 'difficult', and we normally meet it in that ubiquitous little word *dukkha*. So contingency and nirvana aren't difficult to understand intellectually, but they're difficult – even painful – because to the uninitiated they're 'overwhelming and terrifying'.

In practising insight meditation, we're not learning a technical skill in order to penetrate through to some esoteric truth. On the contrary, we're adopting a moral and existential stance in order to seek intimacy with 'the impermanent, tragic and empty aspects of life', which in turn opens up new emotional and aesthetic possibilities.

As the *Satipaṭṭhāna sutta* relates, 'paying embodied attention to life leads to a falling away of habitual patterns, which leads to nirvanic moments when we realize the freedom to respond to life unconditioned by our [self-centred] longings and fears, which [in turn] opens up the possibility of living sanely in this world' (*After Buddhism*, pp.239–40).

In the next session we'll start with section 5 of this chapter, and take the everyday sublime off in a slightly different direction.

Questions for study

1. There are numerous and varying English translations of the word *satipaṭṭhāna*: 'the establishing of mindfulness', 'the foundations of mindfulness', 'the focuses of awareness', and 'the arousing of mindfulness'. In this context, Stephen translates it as 'grounding of mindfulness'. In your opinion, how well does this translation fit here?

2. In his opening paragraph, Stephen lists many meditation practices that are of no interest to him. Have any of these ever been of interest to you? If so, how has your attitude towards them changed over time? To what extent do you agree or disagree with Stephen's view that 'Meditation is about embracing what is happening to this organism as it touches its environment in this moment'?

3. What was your most recent experience of 'the sublime', as the Romantic poets used the term? If you tried to convey the experience to another person, how did you go about it and how successful do you think you were?

4. How do you feel, intellectually, about the concept of the 'everyday sublime'? How do you feel, experientially, about the everyday sublime? Have there been times in your life when you have felt particularly tuned in to (or particularly blind to) the experience of the everyday sublime?

5. What new emotional and aesthetic possibilities have opened up for you through your practice of meditation? If you don't yet have an answer to this, do you have the confidence that such a practice will eventually open up the possibility of living more sanely in this world?

♄ Session twelve:
Doubt and imagination

In the last session, we dealt with the first four sections of chapter nine of Stephen Batchelor's *After Buddhism*: the chapter entitled 'The everyday sublime'. To recap: we saw how, for the author, the nub of dharmic meditation is the uncovering – the realisation – of the everyday sublime.

'The sublime' refers to experiences that are so beautiful, amazing or downright terrifying that they escape our capacity to describe or depict them. Many people might call such experiences 'mystical'. And that's okay, as long as we can awaken to the mystical (or the 'sublime') in our *everyday* experience, instead of seeing the sublime as something grandiose and *apart from* our everyday experience.

To awaken to the everyday sublime we need to cultivate a relationship with it in the form of an ethical path and an existential vision of 'the impermanent, tragic and empty aspects of life'. ('Empty' in the dharmic sense: empty of self.) So in practising insight meditation we're not learning a technical skill that will allow us to penetrate through to some supposed esoteric truth. Rather, we're abandoning our habitual, know-it-all-already, dulling approach to everyday experience and dharma practice.

We're opening the heart and mind to new emotional and aesthetic possibilities inherent in that everyday experience. We can then seize the freedom to respond to life unconditioned by ingrained and self-centred longings and fears. We can open up the possibility of living more sanely in this world.

Now let's tackle the rest of chapter nine, from section 5.

Dharmic aesthetics and doubt

Stephen acknowledges the Korean Sŏn school – in which he practised as a monk for four years – as one of his three outstanding formative influences (along with the Pali canon and his earlier training as a Tibetan monk). Together with its cognate schools in China and Japan, Sŏn has long valued aesthetic experience and the arts, and has melded dharma practice with architecture, sculpture, poetry, calligraphy, pottery, brush-painting and martial arts. It combines this emphasis with its central commitment to doubt as the driving force of dharma practice.

Thus doubt – or 'scepticism' in the western tradition – goes to the core of its meditation practice. Its starting point is a koan (or 'public case' or precedent). The most common koan in Korea is the question, 'What is this?'. It arises from a brief recorded dialogue between the great sixth patriarch of Ch'an, Huineng, and a novice disciple called Huairang. It's their first encounter, after Huairang has walked all the way from Mt Song in northern China, to Huineng's monastery in the country's south. The record of their meeting goes like this:

'Where have you come from?' Huineng asks.
'I've come from Mt Song.'
'But what is this thing and how did it get here?'
Huairang is speechless.

As Stephen comments:

Huineng opens the exchange with a polite enquiry and then subverts it. Without warning, he shifts from conventional chit-chat to an existential challenge, which undermines Huairang's complacency, leaving him exposed, vulnerable and dumb. The text continues with the terse comment: 'Huairang spent eight years in the monastery.' At the end of this period, he returns to the Patriarch and announces that he has an answer:

> Huineng: 'What is this?'
> Huairang: 'To say it is like something misses the point.'

The entire exchange boils down to the simple question: 'What is this?' As is clear from the dialogue, this question is not about Huairang's 'place' but about his 'ground'. Huineng has little, if any, interest in learning facts or details about his interlocutor's *place* in the world: where he lives, where he has travelled from, where he is going. He directs his questioning to Huairang's *ground*: the sheer contingency of the young monk's being there at all: 'What is this thing and how did it get here?' (pp.244–245)

Stephen goes on to explain that 'What is this?' is an uncompromising inquiry into what is going on at any given moment. It throws us straight into the mystery that life is occurring at all – that is, the everyday sublime. Its flip side is the sceptic's refrain: 'I don't know,' hence the Sŏn ideal of 'the don't-know mind'.

After eight years in the monastery Huairang gets it right: no stock answer will do. 'The point' is to cultivate a sensibility which can respond to the immediacy of our unfolding lives free from preconceived opinions and jaded dismissals. This is what dharmic doubt is driving at. It's 'a psychosomatic condition of astonishment and bafflement rather than a discursive mental process' (p.246). We can trace it back to the three questions that the Buddha-to-be posed to himself as a youth: 'What is the delight of life? What is the tragedy of life? What is the emancipation of life?'

The Buddha's verses on 'the sage' – a metaphor for being optimally human, 'a true person' – point to the sensibility in question:

He lets go of one position without taking another –
he's not defined by what he knows.
Nor does he join a dissenting faction –
he assumes no view at all.

He's not lured into the blind alleys
of *it is* and *it is not, this world* and *the next* –
for he lacks those commitments
that make people ponder and seize hold of teachings (p.248).

We have our own converging sceptical tradition in the west, going back to the Greek Pyrrho of Elis, born just 40 years after the Buddha. Like the ancient Greek philosophers in general, for him philosophy wasn't just armchair speculation, but something to be lived and breathed – to be *practised*. His followers formed communities which practised according to the ethic and sensibility of not believing anything that wasn't immediately apparent. Which left them free to respond spontaneously to every moment and contingency.

Institutionalisation

Towards the end of the chapter, Stephen raises two significant issues about the form dharma practice might take as it puts down roots in the west. The first of these issues has to do with institutions. During the Buddha's life, dharma practice did not rely on institutions, but rather informal circles of practitioners. Many dharma communities around the western world today work in the same way.

But in between his time and ours, dharma practice and practitioners (or 'Buddhists') have been massively institutionalised. Institutions often breed bad habits: dogmatism, hierarchies, authoritarianism, patriarchy, career paths, orthodoxies and orthopraxes, and formal techniques for practice – each one usually marketed as 'the one true way'. Institutions are thus unfriendly to the kind of freewheeling scepticism that the Buddha and the Sŏn school (among others) advocate. They leave no room for doubt.

In the pre-digital age, the dharma might not have survived at all without its institutions, even if they have often grossly bent it out of shape. But now information and communication technologies allow us to find each other and ply the dharma tradition without becoming hostages to institutions.

The paradox of the mindfulness movement

The second issue Stephen raises at the end of this chapter is the paradoxical mindfulness movement. As far back as the late nineteenth century, with the dawn of the psychology discipline as such, some westerners hailed Buddhism as 'the scientific religion' because it – unlike literal believers in the book of Genesis – didn't argue with the new evolutionary biology. These westerners even spoke of Buddhism as 'the science of the mind', since it focused on the workings of the mind rather than those of God. The mindfulness movement and today's neuroscientific interest in brain changes during meditation have revived Buddhism's science-friendly credentials.

Stephen worries about the current tendency to instrumentalise the dharma and treat meditation as a problem-solving technique, rather than as the cultivation of a sensibility that engages with the wonder, tragedy and emancipation of human life as a whole. So all talk of the quantifiable 'effectiveness' of meditation in attaining any particular clinical result cuts across its original dharmic thrust. Likewise reducing it to technical issues. 'Meditation is more usefully compared to the ongoing practice of an art than the development of a technical ability' (p.257).

But then he ends the chapter with a spirited *defence* of the mind-

fulness movement against the Buddhist traditionalists' charge that
it represents a 'dumbing down' of the dharma:

> This elitist objection fails to recognise how Buddhism has been
> dumbing itself down ever since it began. It is doubtful that those
> who condemn the mindfulness movement on such grounds
> would likewise condemn the practice of millions of Buddhists
> that consists in repeating over and over again the name of the
> mythical Buddha Amitabha or the title of the *Lotus Sutra* (p.258).

Today's mindfulness movement is doing far better than that,
Stephen suggests. It's getting people to come together and sit on
chairs and cushions to observe their breath. Even in the complete
absence of Buddhist doctrine, many people find these exercises
deeply rewarding in helping them live balanced and meaningful
lives.

> Rather than complain about the 'dumbing down' of the dharma,
> Buddhists need to rise to the challenge of articulating a philo-
> sophically coherent and ethically integrated vision of life that is
> no longer tied to the religious dogmas and institutions of Asian
> Buddhism. In this way, perhaps, they might help encourage the
> dawning of a culture of awakening, which may or may not call
> itself 'Buddhist' (p.259).

Questions for study

1. The word 'doubt' is crucial in this session. Can you clearly state the difference between the everyday use of the word, as in 'They say it's going to rain later, but I doubt that,' and the dharmic use of the word, for example 'in Korean Sŏn, doubt is the driving force of dharma practice'?

2. What do you make of Huaijang's (eventual) answer to 'What is this?', namely 'To say that it is like something misses the point'? Why do you think it took him eight years to come up with this response? How might things have gone differently if he had been tipped off on first entering the monastery that this was 'a good answer' to give to Huineng?

3. The 'What is this?' practice could be described as cultivating an appreciation of not-knowing. How does this differ from the fearful curiosity kind of not-knowing which may possess us when, for example, we wake up in the middle of the night and hear an unfamiliar sound?

4. Does it sound to you like 'the sage' is being even-handed in applying his scepticism? What would one-sided scepticism look like, and why might 'a true person' do well to avoid this common form of scepticism?

5. With modern communications technologies arguably making worldwide social networking a reality, it is now possible for geographically remote individuals to form dharma communities. Reflect on your experience of this kind of digital sangha, and evaluate its pros and cons in avoiding the pitfalls of institutionalisation.

6. How concerned are you about the phenomenon of meditation-as-medicine, where it is prescribed as a problem-solving technique? From your perspective, where is the mindfulness movement headed? What do you think it will look like in five years? Ten years? What might people be saying, in retrospect, about Mindfulness Based Stress Reduction and institutional western Buddhism fifty years from now?

∅ Session thirteen:
Ānanda: the attendant

We've now reached chapter 10 of Stephen Batchelor's *After Buddhism*, the title of which refers to the best-known figure in the discourses after the Buddha himself – Ānanda, on whom our very reception of them depends. He was the chief memorist of the early tradition in its oral period. Thanks to him and his phenomenal eye and ear for detail, as well as memory, we can not only read a plausible account of what the Buddha said, but in what sociohistorical context, and in what imperfect, shaky, dusty human world he said it.

We've already seen in earlier sessions how Stephen extrapolates the stories of rounded individuals (Mahānama, Pasenadi, Sunakhatta, Jīvaka, and now Ānanda), rather than once more lionising the usual 'depersonalised saints' from Central Casting who could afford to ignore the social and political upheavals that attended the birth of the dharma.

As Stephen points out, this world that Ānanda shared with his first cousin Gotama (aka the Buddha) was a far cry from the mythic world of Indian epics, from the Mahābarāta to the gorgeous Mahāyāna sutras. The characters who populate his account have recognisable human traits and flaws, and the Buddha himself retains his human frailty. If we look closely into Ānanda's narratives, and others' narratives that follow after the Buddha's death, he himself also emerges as a rounded character.

So this chapter is by no means all about him, but extends into what he recounts about schisms and ruptures in the early dharma community, and in that regard, about the Buddha's death, which the later tradition masked with mythological elements.

Meet Ānanda

You might say that Ānanda was born well-connected. He was a first cousin of both the Buddha and Mahānama (whom we met in session three), as well as being the much younger half-brother of Devadatta of infamy (whom we'll meet shortly). Ānanda was the same age as the Buddha's son Rāhula, and so was 30 years younger than the Buddha himself.

He joined the Buddha's mendicant followers when aged twenty. Five years later he took on the role of the Buddha's attendant, which he retained until the Buddha's death aged 80 (when Ānanda himself was around 50). He's a vital link between the Buddha's generation and the one that postdated the Buddha's death around 400 BCE. Apart from his 25 years of directly witnessing every teaching the then mature Buddha gave, he collected the oral records of the master's earlier teachings.

Like the Buddha, Ānanda was socially progressive. During the Buddha's life and within his movement, the perennial cleavage (still alive and well today) developed between:

- those who shunned hierarchy, rigidity around rules, and fanaticism in the cultivation of core spiritual values; and
- those who sought to channel their spiritual and religious commitments into precisely these preoccupations.

In short: this is the endless struggle between progress and re-action. This chapter of *After Buddhism* contains two vital examples of it, as we'll see.

On one notable occasion, the Buddha played catchup with Ānanda in this regard, though Stephen doesn't mention it in this chapter. When the Buddha's aunt and stepmother, Mahāpajāpatī, together with several other women, asks him to ordain them into the mendicant community, the Buddha initially refuses. We can speculate why he might have done so. He's already controversial enough for bucking the caste system; is he now going to take on the gender system as well?

In any event, Ānanda challenges his decision. Does the Exalted One believe that women have a lesser spiritual potential than men? he asks. No, the Exalted One believes no such thing. And so? asks Ānanda. Ask them to come back in, replies the Exalted One, and duly does as asked. I hardly have to remind you that large swathes of the religious world are still today struggling to get to this point. It's also the only recorded case of the Buddha being persuaded to change his mind.

On other occasions, including after the Buddha's death, Ānanda went into bat for women dharma practitioners, and sometimes came in for hard criticism from reactionaries for so doing. Perhaps he should be celebrated as one of the very first feminists in recorded history.

How were the dharma and community to survive the Buddha's death?
When the Buddha was around 55 years old, he seems to have turned his mind to the question of how his teaching and his practice community would survive his death. He complained of feeling old and sick – intimations of mortality. But the increasingly unstable political and social conditions may have also fuelled these concerns. Clearly others were asking the same questions, most notably the Buddha's cousin Devadatta, also a long-time mendicant follower.

In the conventional, commentarial accounts, Devadatta comes

across as a caricatured baddie – the Buddhist world's answer to Judas Iscariot. The canon presents him as much more interesting, and a recurring type in religious life more generally. He's driven by an urge to take control, and his main stock-in-trade is exaggerated asceticism, rule-boundedness, and the cultish tendency to cut his followers off from all outside contact. (Here is one of the two 'dead ends' the Buddha named in his first discourse. No doubt we can all think of other familiar examples of Devadatta's syndrome among today's Abrahamic religions!) Perhaps he's also genuinely worried that the Buddha's leadership of the community is too lax, and he'll leave it unsustainable when he dies.

Devadatta's first ploy is to suggest to the Buddha (72 years old at the time) in public that he's over the hill; he should retire and pass the leadership of the sangha over to him, Devadatta. The Buddha's reply to this unsubtle move was even less subtle: he has no intention of passing the leadership to anyone, not even to his most realised disciples and close friends, Sāriputta or Moggallāna, *'let alone to a lickspittle like you,'* he tells Devadatta.

Thus rebuffed and humiliated, Devadatta sets out to subvert the Buddha's authority by spreading it around that the Buddha allows his followers too much freedom and doesn't enforce strict austerity on them, including total withdrawal from society. How could such a slack teacher bring his followers to liberation? On this basis Devadatta splits the community, establishes his own ascetic faction, and in the process encourages the reigning king's son Ajātasattu to commit patricide and regicide. Exit one of the Buddha's chief patrons, King Bimbisāra of Magadha.

This is the first of a series of setbacks and tragedies that mark the Buddha's last years and cast a pall over Ānanda's life as well. The Buddha loses perhaps a substantial part of his following to Devadatta, and Magadha is no longer a safe haven for him and his remaining community. In the next eight years up to his death, Sāriputta and Moggallāna predecease him in quick succession, his other royal patron in Kosala, Pasenadi, is deposed and dies, his other much-loved cousin, Mahānama, perishes in a vain attempt to stop Pasenadi's successor slaughtering their people, the Sakiyans.

Through all these vicissitudes the Buddha's determination to prevent his community ever coming under the thrall of another authority figure remains firm. For Ānanda, however, the sense of insecurity is too much, and he begs the Buddha to address the problem of leadership, cohesion and survival of the dharma.

In highly significant terms, the Buddha flatly refuses to anoint a successor. He has taught the true dharma, holding nothing back, he tells Ānanda. There are no esoteric teachings to hand on to a successor. His followers already have it all at their fingertips. When he dies, they should be *islands unto themselves*, practising the dharma according to their own personal integrity, independent of others.

So they have no need of a fixed code of rules: 'Abolish the minor rules,' he admonishes Ānanda, since those that he's set up simply address particular circumstances that will change over time. The dharma alone should be their refuge; the community has no need of a leader. All this is implicit, too, in his very last words: 'Things fall apart; tread the path with care (*appamāda*).'

The contrast between this vision of spiritual community and Devadatta's could hardly be stronger. If the Buddha had any magical powers at all, they came down to foreseeing the development of the papacy, the patriarchates and the caliphates. He does everything in his power to prevent his tradition from degenerating in that way.

Tragically, very soon after the Buddha's death, a particularly forceful control freak arrives on the scene and assumes command. This is Kassapa, whose conception of spiritual practice and community is much closer to Devadatta's than to the Buddha's and Ānanda's.

He goes out of his way to humiliate and isolate Ānanda. He enshrines the existing monastic code in its entirety as unchangeable, and marginalises and subordinates women. Kassapa is, after all, to the manor born, coming from a Brahmin family with a culture of dogmatism, hierarchy and misogyny. And Ānanda can't stand up to him.

But both set their stamp on the dharma's development. By and large, it institutionalised according to Kassapa's predilections. However, at the first council, held within months of the Buddha's death, Ānanda recited the entire corpus of the Buddha's discourses (except for some that later found their way into the Vinaya) so that many others could learn them by rote.

It's thanks to Ānanda that we have the discourses we've been studying all these years, with their subversive edge turned towards conventional institutionalised Buddhism. He also lived to a ripe old age, and attracted his own following.

Anyone can read the Buddha's refusal to appoint a successor, and his enthronement instead of the care and integrity of the individual's own dharma practice. Buddhist institutions have been responsible for much mischief, but in all this time no one has managed to set himself up as a Buddhist pope.

Questions for study

1. When you picture Gotama, the Buddha, in your mind's eye, what do you see? Try drawing Gotama and Ānanda; the focus here is not on artistic proficiency, but to give yourself the opportunity to reflect on your received views of the people referred to in the Pali canon. If you find you have placed any of the characters on a particularly high pedestal, try imagining them in an everyday scenario (eating a meal or stubbing their toe).

2. Based on your previous actions, where would you place yourself on the spectrum between the poles of progressiveness and conservatism? How about those that you know well in your community? Is there anyone you know well who takes a very different approach to your own, and how do you feel about them? Have you witnessed the struggle between progress and reaction in a dharma community, from within or without? Is there a middle way between the two?

3. How do you feel about the incident where the Buddha refers to Devadatta as a 'lickspittle'? If this description is too mild to generate some kind of reaction from you, try substituting a more salty translation. Do you feel the urge to rush to Gotama's defence against some slur on his character that you might have imagined? How is it that this dialogue, which is not characteristic of the serene stereotype of an enlightened being, survived the test of time and was included in the canon?

4. Would it have been better if Gotama had appointed a successor to lead his community after his death? In what ways might this have been a wise move, and in what terms would you define 'success' in this context?

5. Around 2,500 years ago we find Ānanda rising to the challenge

of bringing gender equality and inclusiveness to the sangha –
the community of dharma practitioners. How well is your own
sangha succeeding in this project?

∅ Session fourteen:
A culture of awakening (part 1)

We've now arrived at chapter 11 – the last substantive chapter – of *After Buddhism*. It too follows the pattern of alternating chapters dealing with specific characters who appear in the Pali canon, and general-topic ones. Last time we met Ānanda; now we start in on 'a culture of awakening' – Stephen Batchelor's characterisation of what the dharma constitutes in essence, and how dharma practice might develop under that rubric in the west.

We'll engage with the first four sections of the chapter (up to p.306) because they have such important implications for how we understand the dharma's relationship to culture in general and western culture in particular. These sections help us to know what we're doing in taking on the dharma in the west. In the next session we'll introduce the rest of the material in chapter 11.

Dharma teaching in the west tends to neglect (or at least drastically underplay) the role that culture and institutions have played in the development of the tradition, from the Buddha's time and place to our own, and how we should articulate the dharma now.

We need to be aware of their roles while we, as practitioners, play our own part in crystallising the dharma in our own lives and societies. Because these two closely intertwined influences – culture and institutions – shape what we think we know, what we take for granted, how we make sense of things, and even what we say and do.

We are children of our culture

Stephen begins the chapter with a quote from the Buddha, from 'The book of the aggregates' (*Khandhasaṃyutta*):

> I do not dispute with the world; rather it is the world that disputes with me. A proponent of the dharma does not dispute with anyone in the world. Of that which the wise (*paṇḍitā*) in the world agree upon as not existing, I too say that it does not exist. And of that which the wise in the world agree upon as existing, I too say that it exists (p.293).

In modern terms, the Buddha is disclaiming omniscience. He's implying that, if you want information on any particular subject, consult an expert. Dr Google, if you like, or Siri. 'The wise in the world' refers to anyone the inquirer regards as authoritative in the area in question. If you want to know how the universe began, ring up an astrophysicist. If you want to know how to avoid eternal hellfire, ask a priest who knows his way around the theological texts in question.

On the one hand, the Buddha is laying out the common sense position. On the other, he's refusing the role of a dogmatic one-stop shop. Which hasn't stopped many of his highly placed followers pontificating on matters far beyond their reach and capacity, and citing the Buddha as the source of their own dogmas.

The categories of 'the wise in the world' have expanded without changing much in the intervening time. The Buddha acknowledged and drew on the expertise of musicologists and physicians, for instance – the equivalent of our scientific establishment today. He also acknowledged the expertise of Brahmin priests in interpreting the Vedas and Upanishads, without drawing on the latter (because they had nothing to do with his own concerns).

But all these inquiries and consultations take place in the *pre-*

existing realm of culture and language. Well may St John begin his gospel with the famous statement: 'In the beginning was the word, and the word was with God, and the word was God.' Words – cultural products – shape our experiences, our understandings of them and their contexts. Our life-worlds. Whoever coined the word 'God' in effect created the deity, who keeps being verbally resuscitated to this day. With all that that implies. As the British poet Kate Tempest put it recently: 'people are killing for gods again.'

The words we use come in bundles – whole languages cradled in whole cultures, which they invoke and reinforce. And those cultures mandate certain myths, conventional understandings, and emphases. So we can't avoid a culture clash when we take a tradition of practice and inquiry developed in ancient India and re-root it in the modern post-Christian west. We are acculturated to make fundamental assumptions about our existence that contradict those of institutionalised Asian Buddhism. The doctrine of karma and rebirth is the central case in point in Stephen's analysis.

Inflexibilities in western culture
Few readers are likely to subscribe to this doctrine as it is conventionally taught. There are compelling reasons for not doing so, ones we don't need to rehearse here yet again. But we do need to inquire into what's going on in our own corner when we refuse this doctrine. We're rejecting it under two major influences on our own culture: (a) the cultural remnants of Abrahamic religion (which had no place for karma and rebirth) in our western languages and folkways; and (b) the hegemony of scientific naturalism and its celebration of 'objective truth'. The latter rests on the so-called correspondence theory of truth (see session 7) whereby a truth-claim stands on its supposed correspondence to the way things ultimately are.

These influences inhibit us from adopting the straightforward pragmatic approach to the culture clash that Stephen implicitly proposes, and the dharma upholds. After all, the first path factor, 'appropriate view' (*sammā ditthi*) refers to a reality construct that supports effective spiritual practice. *One that works!* Not one that comes out of scientific journals with the 'objective truth' accolade. Conversely, wrong view (*micchā ditthi*) is one that obstructs or misleads our practice.

> For the majority of Buddhists over time [Stephen writes at p.296] belief in reincarnation has served as a pragmatic rather than dogmatic way of understanding oneself and the world. As a functional belief embedded within their culture and society, it works well enough for it not to be seriously doubted.

Indian religious culture sets practice over belief, while Abrahamic religions do the precise opposite. For the latter, *belief* is all important – so much so that in the west, 'belief' (or 'creed' – the same thing) is a synonym for religion itself. Just because traditional Buddhists retain karma and rebirth as a working assumption doesn't mean they actually *believe* it in the same way our ancestors *believed* the propositions in (some iteration of) the Christian *Creed*, and we ourselves *believe* (as absolute objective truth) that the earth revolves around the sun.

The flexible appropriation of the dharma in the west thus comes up against major obstacles in the new host culture, ones that have nothing to do with the apparent implausibility of the old Indian world view. The two most important obstacles relate back to the two major influences on our culture already mentioned: (a) the continuing fetish around belief (or so-called 'objective truth') at the expense of practice, and (b) the dominance of scientistic culture over interpretive modes of thought.

Interpretive vs. scientistic mindsets

Interestingly, the secular Buddhist tendency itself illustrates these problems of cultural adaptation internationally, as I witnessed at first hand at a conference on the subject at the Barre Center for Buddhist Studies in Massachusetts in March 2013. The USA distinguishes itself from the rest of the west, among other ways, in the surviving intensity of its religious culture and its Christian self-assertion. 'Secular' seems to be a dirty word there, a bit like 'communist', and so American secular Buddhists tend to bring up the heavy artillery to defend themselves from aggressive religiosity.

The heavy artillery in question is natural science, so the battle rages over the plausibility of biblical assertions, the existence of God, and so on. The Buddha becomes an artilleryman, and Buddhism is once again 'the scientific religion' that it was in the nineteenth century when the Christian establishment crossed swords with evolutionary biologists in defence of creationism. But now neuroscience is a major piece of new ordnance to fire at the 'god botherers'. The issue is: whose account of objective truth is going to win, making this at bottom a fight between fundamentalisms.

The small minority of us in Barre who weren't Americans found all this odd. We came from much more secular societies and in the main we were far more interested in interpretive (as opposed to scientistic) modes of thought in fostering the dharma in the west.

Pragmatism, phenomenology, existentialism and hermeneutics seemed to some of us to provide useful pathways, ones that have strong affinities with the Buddha's own teachings. Humans are not just conscious beings but acculturated, self-interpreting and volitional ones too – ones always confronted with questions of meaning and the path to a meaningful life. As dharma students we're on home ground here.

∅

In the next session we'll look at the positive side of the cultural challenge: the dharma as the kernel in a culture of awakening. The main point to take away from this session is that we need to avoid getting our knickers in a twist over conundrums of belief and so-called truth that our own culture – for historical reasons – tends to fuss about. Instead, we can enter into the spirit of the Buddha's own refusal to get dragged into issues of metaphysical 'truth', and instead pursue what works.

Questions for study

1. The opening quote from Chapter 11 of *After Buddhism* contains the statement, 'A proponent of the dharma does not dispute with anyone in the world'. What do you think is meant by this sentence in this context? How would you explain it to someone who understands it to mean that Buddhists should not argue with people?

2. If you were asked to state a time in your life when it has been most obvious that words shaped your experiences, your understandings of them and their contexts, what is the first thing that comes to mind? Have you ever been in a situation where another person has completely failed to understand the importance of this kind of cultural and linguistic context? Perhaps that other person was a child, or an adult who has lived their life within very small horizons. Have you ever been immersed in another culture and language such that the connection between culture and perception has been made more obvious?

3. Consider this extract from David Chapman's blog 'Vividness'[vividness.live/2011/06/16/the-making-of-buddhist-modernism]:

> 'Buddhist modernism has been successful because it makes sense to westerners. That's not surprising: much of it is our own culture, repackaged and passed back to us. Familiar ideas about individual access to ultimate truth (a core theme of Protestantism), social justice, and emotional health are dressed up with Sanskrit, Pali, or Tibetan words, and supported with highly selective quotations from Buddhist scripture. That makes them intriguingly exotic, yet comfortably unthreatening.'

Making the dharma appropriate to modern westerners would seem to require making it familiar enough to be accessible, but not so familiar that it fails to challenge the status quo. To what extent do you think Stephen has succeeded in charting a middle way between these two dead ends?

4. The western emphasis on belief in religion is obvious if one searches the internet with the phrase, 'What do Buddhists believe?' (Try it!) As an example, read the Simple English Wikipedia article on Buddhism[https://simple.wikipedia.org/wiki/Buddhism] and then imagine how you would feel towards a peer who said that they 'believed' all the things that it is claimed there that a Buddhist believes. Putting aside your views on individual liberty and toleration, how much respect do you think you have for such a person? Do you think that such Buddhists exist, or are they a straw man of your own creation?

5. How do you feel about the promotion of Buddhism as 'the scientific religion'? Don't be sidetracked by the justification (or lack of justification) for such a view. Focus instead on investigating how you feel about Buddhism being 'sold' in this way.

⌀ Session fifteen:
A culture of awakening (part 2)

In the last session, we looked at the first four sections of chapter 11 in Stephen Batchelor's *After Buddhism*. The chapter, called 'A culture of awakening', presents a manifesto for a possible development of dharma practice and of dharma-practising communities in the west. We started by pointing to the formative influence of the reigning cultures and institutions in specific times and places on how the dharma and its practice have later been conventionally understood elsewhere. This is the problem we face in the west today: conventional Buddhism comes to us inflected in culturally unhelpful ways.

Everyone in any particular human community shares a culture which we can compare to the operating system in our computers: the culture (and especially the language embedded in it) shapes and creates meaning for us, empowering us to think, communicate, and act. Like everything else in our lived world, cultures and institutions change and grow, responding to changing conditions. Or they stagnate and wither. Just like plants.

In adapting and rooting the dharma in the west, we need a sense of how it developed elsewhere, the cultures from which it comes to us, and what in our own inherited western culture can help – or deflect – us as we seek to make the most of it in our own situation. In this regard we noted the exaggerated significance of *belief as such* in western religious culture, and the importance for us – in looking at the working assumptions of 'traditional' Buddhists – of adopting a pragmatist stance towards truth claims.

Appropriate view (the first path factor) is the view that guides effective practice, not something claiming ultimate truth. So, for instance, we really don't need to engage with the debate over the ultimate truth-value of traditional assumptions about karma and rebirth. At the same time we need to see why we ourselves get hung up on such disputes – because we've inherited a concept of ultimate scientific truth we can trace back to the earlier idea of ultimate religious truth. The search for ultimates deflects us from effective practice – a point the Buddha made over and over, for instance in the parable of the poisoned arrow.

The pragmatics of the traditional teachings

So in the latter sections of this chapter, Stephen takes us through the pragmatics (rather than the metaphysics) of the traditional teachings about karma, rebirth and the legend of Māra, the personification of death and evil. Karma takes us into the heart of conditionality, and our place in it: *thoughts, words and actions have consequences.*

This is still news to many of us. Or once again news. In the western world we face a narcissism epidemic, and one of the narcissist's key characteristics is the inability to connect the dots that reveal the patterns of cause and effect, and thus of personal responsibility.

How about rebirth? The Pali term for it, *punabhava,* literally means 'again-becoming'. In other words, *repetitive existence* – a nice expression for our habitual patterns of reactivity, which tend to diminish and exhaust our lives in unfree same old, same old holding patterns. We're not fully alive when these patterns capture us. They condemn us to a sort of living death.

That's where Māra comes in. He personifies this repetitive way of 'living and partly living', as TS Eliot put it. He stands for what diminishes us, what stops us from flourishing. What puts us into a spiritual twilight zone. (Stephen expanded on this analysis in his earlier book, *Living with the devil*.) But let's not write him off by mixing him up with our Judaeo-Christian concept of the devil. The pragmatics of Māra goes far deeper than that.

Buddha and Māra aren't polar opposites. Buddha couldn't be Buddha without Māra, who establishes the problem that Buddha must solve in order to become Buddha. Together these two figures complete the picture of our conflicted humanity and the potential for awakening that inheres in it.

In the Pali canon, Māra as the subtle tempter regularly reappears to the Buddha and his advanced disciples to test their self-reflective alertness – to check that they haven't deluded themselves in their breakout from repetitive existence. They pass the test each time by saying, 'I know you, Māra,' whereupon it's game over until next time.

Knowing Mara is essential to our practice of the four tasks (or 'the fourfold task'). It leads to the often fleeting but returning experience of nirvanic freedom that the third task enjoins us to realise. We can't do it without Māra, the keeper of our human condition, our dark dharmic coach who threatens to lure us back into samsaric bondage.

By the same token Māra, as the personification of death and the human condition, must accompany our sense of Buddha as the personification of human flourishing and awakening. In his *Being and time*, Martin Heidegger emphasises essentially the same point by including – in his list of key aspects of being human – being-towards-death. His point was that in order to maximise our human potential, we must remain grounded, among other ways, by remaining conscious of our *finitude* (that is, our mortality, vulnerability and limitations). The very opposite of narcissistic grandiosity.

The communitarian imperative

But we can't awaken all by ourselves, as isolated individuals. That's why we need a culture of awakening. We need culture (including language) to function as humans, just as our computers need operating systems. But culture and language (and operating systems) are communal products that require constant communal support and upgrades to remain fit for purpose.

At bottom, a community isn't an empirical sociological group, but rather a *process* whereby we humans come together, form relationships, communicate and harmonise our efforts to get things done. Things we couldn't possibly do as isolated individuals – including surviving at all. Let alone finding meaning. To say nothing of awakening. In Heidegger's terms, community is the essential human practice of being-with-others, to further a common project.

We come together in community, interacting with each other under the auspices of something called a *sangha*. A sangha is a communal practice dedicated to individuals' mutual support in pursuit of a central value: awakening in the Buddha's dispensation. As with any other process of community, we need to think about how we should communicate with each other, and how we should associate with each other so as to advance our shared central values.

In other words, we need to think about generating and participating in a *culture of awakening* appropriate to the resources of the current, wider ambient culture, and the kinds of human beings into which it has moulded us. Paradoxically, though, our starting point is in an ancient Pali word that originally referred to a tribal council of elders. A sangha was the alternative practice of decision-making and coordination to absolute one-man rule (literal 'monarchy', more familiarly known as tyranny).

The Buddha himself grew up in the sanghic political community of the Sakiyans. Since his father 'chaired' the council, he knew exactly how and why this model worked. Not surprisingly, when he attracted followers as a spiritual teacher, he adopted the model (and even the word *sangha* itself) for the way his small, local groups of followers should practise community.

These days the general model in question has a very long pedigree which elucidates its ramifications. As usual, the Greeks (not least the Athenians) were onto it at the same time as the Buddha. Here in the west we inherit their version – suitably enhanced from to time, for instance by the later insistence on inclusiveness – under the rubric of *civic republicanism*. Its basic value is freedom understood as self-rule, or self-determination. The practitioners meet and speak as equals, free of power inequalities and other constraints, and in this way make all the vital decisions that no other power-holder can thwart.

The contemporary German philosopher Jürgen Habermas calls the process involved here the *'ideal speech situation'*. It's one in which there are no barriers to entry, and the participants discuss their mutual affairs as equals, free of all manipulative or 'coercive' influences, as they work towards an eventual consensus.

The eclipse of the Buddha's model of sangha

Alas, soon after his death, the Buddha's model of spiritual community was overthrown by its opposite – the exclusivist, hierarchical, authoritarian model that became the template for Buddhist monastic life. As we saw two sessions ago, Stephen relates the story of how Kassapa seized the reins and brutally marginalised Ānanda to achieve this outcome – fortunately without expunging the Buddha's and Ānanda's antithetical sanghic values from the canonical record.

With Kassapa's coup, Buddhist institutions came to adopt many of the features that western monotheistic religion took on: hierarchy, dogma, exclusion of women, a professional priestly class, deification of icons and demonisation of ordinary human traits, the promise of 'transcendence' to blissful post-human or superhuman states for the compliant, and seriously scary postmortem destinations for the non-compliant.

Retrieving the ancient city

Stephen sets the Buddha's parable of the ancient city centre stage as the clearest, most succinct statement of the Buddha's own sanghic values, and perhaps of his whole mission as a spiritual teacher.

Here the Buddha compares himself to a wanderer in a jungle who stumbles on the ruins of a remarkably commodious ancient city. He persuades the local authorities to restore it, and sometime later it's once again home to a growing community, bustling with life. The citizens of this city have no master or priests. Their harmony, purposefulness and flourishing come from their practice of the four tasks. Reading between the lines, we can assume that they manage their common affairs by exercising civic-republican virtues, equality and inclusiveness, and the ethic of the ideal speech situation.

The restored city is not a utopia. It's not a communion of saints or a six-star resort reserved for glittering bodhisattvas or austere old arahants. Nor is there any institutional template to rigidly follow. Rather, it's a human-friendly place that provides broad hints about how we might develop our own sanghic life, and the culture of awakening we might generate in the process.

Questions for study

1. What do you think of the analogy between a culture and an operating system on a computer? How helpful is this comparison in understanding the way in which we approach everyday life? With the support and upgrades that an operating system needs in mind, is culture more like an open-source code or a proprietary system controlled by vested interests such as Apple or Microsoft? Are there any significant ways in which the analogy between cultures and operating systems fails?

2. How does the suggestion that there is an 'ultimate truth' sit with you? Do you have a tendency to get hung up on disputes about ultimate truth, even if you take a pragmatic approach to appropriate view (*sammā diṭṭhi*) in dharma practice? Do you know anyone who is particularly fervent in their belief in an ultimate truth of one kind or another? How has this helped and/ or hindered them in dealing with the existential tribulations of life? If you were a believer like this in the past, how do you think you later let go of the 'ultimate truth' in question?

3. How useful is the concept of karma for us today? Do you think we really need to be reminded that 'thoughts, words and actions have consequences'? Do you have any strong feelings about the extent of individual responsibility? How does your viewpoint here influence the ethical choices you make in your life?

4. Do you experience any conflict between the practice of 'knowing Mara' and the (likely) culturally ingrained imperative to 'not think sinful thoughts'? Is there any practice or approach you have found useful in integrating the archetypes personified by Buddha and Mara?

5. What advantages do you see in considering community as a process rather than simply a group with a defined membership? In your experience of being part of a number of overlapping communities, what is the closest any of them have come to realising an 'ideal speech situation'? What factors have helped in achieving it? If you are part of a community that is a long way from an ideal speech situation, what factors might be holding it back?

6. In the Christian gospels, one of Jesus' recurring themes was that 'the kingdom of God' is at hand. The interpretation of this message seems to vary according to whoever is doing the interpreting. If you are familiar with a particular Christian interpretation of the kingdom of God (also known as the 'kingdom of heaven'), how does it compare with the Buddha's parable about the restoration of the ancient city?

⌀ Session sixteen:
Ten theses of secular dharma

'A culture of awakening' is the last substantive chapter of Stephen Batchelor's *After Buddhism*. It ends on p.321 with his 'ten theses of secular dharma' which – in the space of a page – distil the practical implications of his book for modern practitioners of (and inquirers into) the Buddha's dharma.

The ten theses also offer readers of this workbook the best conclusion imaginable. The theses also function as discussion questions. To what extent can each of us – and our practice community as a whole – subscribe to these propositions? Where does the shoe pinch? And why? Is our resistance intellectually and emotionally genuine? Or does it arise from a reluctance to abandon comforting myths, or positions we've publicly affirmed in the past?

Here come the ten theses. Now it's over to you.

1. A secular Buddhist is one who is committed to the practice of the dharma for the sake of this world alone.

2. The practice of the dharma consists of four tasks: to embrace suffering, let go of reactivity, behold the ceasing of reactivity, and cultivate an integrated way of life.

3. All human beings, irrespective of gender, race, sexual orientation, disability, nationality and religion can practise

these four tasks. Each person, in each moment, has the potential to be more awake, responsive and free.

4. The practice of the dharma is as much concerned with how one speaks, acts and works in the public realm as with how one performs spiritual exercises in private.

5. The dharma serves the needs of people at specific times and places. Each form the dharma assumes is a transient human creation, contingent upon the historical, cultural, social and economic conditions that generated it.

6. The practitioner honours the dharma teachings that have been passed down through different traditions while seeking to enact them creatively in ways appropriate to the world as it is now.

7. The community of practitioners is formed of autonomous persons who mutually support each other in the cultivation of their paths. This network of like-minded individuals respects the equality of all members while honouring the specific knowledge and expertise each person brings.

8. A practitioner is committed to an ethics of care, founded on empathy, compassion, and love for all creatures who have evolved on this earth.

9. Practitioners seek to understand and diminish the structural violence of societies and institutions as well as the roots of violence that are present in themselves.

10. A practitioner of the dharma aspires to nurture a culture of awakening that finds its inspiration in Buddhist and non-Buddhist, religious and secular sources alike.

⌀ References

Batchelor, Stephen (2004) *Living with the devil: a meditation on good and evil* (New York: Riverhead)

Batchelor, Stephen (2015) *After Buddhism: rethinking the dharma for a secular age* (Yale University Press: New Haven & London)

Bazzano, Manu (ed., 2014) *After mindfulness: new perspectives on psychology and meditation* (London: Palgrave/Macmillan)

Cupitt, Don (1997) *After God: The future of religion* (London: Weidenfeld & Nicolson)

Eagleton, Terry (2014) *Culture and the death of God* (New Haven & London: Yale University Press)

Heidegger, Martin ([1927] 2008) *Being and time* (John Macquarrie & Edward Robinson transl. New York & London: Harper Perennial)

Massimo, Michael (2014) 'A view of the earth', in Catherine Burns (ed.) *The moth* (London: Serpent's Tail)

Ñāṇavīra Thera ([1987] 2001) *Clearing the path: writings of Ñāṇavīra Thera* (1960-1965) (Two volumes. Dehiwali, Sri Lanka: Buddhist Cultural Centre)

Siff, Jason (2008) *Seeking nibbana in Sri Lanka* (Kathmandu: Vajra Publications)

Taylor, Charles (2007) *A secular age* (Cambridge MA & London: Belknap)

Vattimo, Gianni (2002) *After Christianity* (New York: Columbia University Press)

Vattimo, Gianni (2011) *A farewell to truth* (New York: Columbia University Press)

⌀ The authors

Winton Higgins

Is a senior teacher for Sydney Insight Meditators and three of its constituent local sanghas. He began practising the dharma in 1987, and has taught insight meditation since 1995, including leading residential retreats. Since 2005 his teaching has increasingly focused on non-formulaic forms of insight meditation, and secular Buddhism. Winton's dharma writings have appeared in Journal of Global Buddhism and at **secularbuddhism.org.nz/ resources/documents/#wh**. He is also an associate of the School of International Studies, University of Technology Sydney, and a novelist. His website is at **wintonhiggins.org**.

Jim Champion

Specialised in theoretical physics to PhD level, and then trained as a secondary school teacher. In 2004, he returned to Hampshire to teach physics. Jim first encountered secular Buddhism in April 2016, and has been practising since then. He is a member of The Middle Way Society, and the international online community Re~Collective.

Ramsey Margolis

Who conceived, shaped and nurtured this book, first experienced meditation in 1995 and has run meditation groups in Wellington from 2000. In 2009, Ramsey set up Aotearoa Buddhist Education Trust and currently chairs the board. A year later, he launched **secularbuddhism.org.nz**, and in 2011 set up Wellington's secular dharma practice community Simply Meditation (now One Mindful Breath), where he teaches meditation and secular Buddhism, runs courses, and mentors individual practitioners.

TUWHIRI

FINDING MEANING IN A DIFFICULT WORLD

A word in te reo Maori, tuwhiri means to disclose, reveal, divulge, make known, or a clue, a means of discovering or disclosing something lost or hidden, a hint, a tip, a pointer.

The Tuwhiri Project Ltd is 100 percent owned by Aotearoa Buddhist Education Trust (ABET), a New Zealand registered charity. As a social enterprise with no investor shareholders and no need to prioritise profit-making, we can focus on our purpose: to help people find meaning in a difficult world.

Tuwhiri is an initiative of Ramsey Margolis and Peter Cowley in Wellington, New Zealand, and Winton Higgins and Margaret Tung in Sydney, Australia. *After Buddhism: a workbook* is our first book and others are on their way. As well as publishing books with a focus on early Buddhism, its retrieval, and secular adaptation to twenty-first century conditions, we will be developing online courses that will help people develop a secular take on the dharma.

We are immensely grateful to all the Tuwhiri Sponsors, Book Supporters and Kickstarter backers who helped breathe life into the aspiration that has become Tuwhiri, financing the production of this book. Also for the time, energy and expertise so generously given to this project by people, communities and organisations in Sydney, Wellington, and elsewhere around the world.

To continue to produce books and develop online courses, we need your help. In New Zealand you can make a charitable donation through ABET for The Tuwhiri Project to 38-9019-0064662-07; to donate by debit card or credit card from any country go to www.abet.org.nz/how-to-donate/.

For more information on The Tuwhiri Project visit www.tuwhiri.nz.

Our Kickstarter donors

This book has been made possible though the generous support of individuals and communities around the world, some of whom choose to remain anonymous, and includes 98 Kickstarter backers. We thank you all.

Tuwhiri Sponsors

Gary Dean • Indonesia
One Mindful Breath • Wellington, New Zealand
Ross Carter-Brown • Christchurch, New Zealand
Steve Lovinger • Barcelona, Spain

Book Supporters

Beaches Sangha • Sydney, Australia
Brad Parks, Sati Sangha teacher-in-training • Santa Barbara CA, USA
Christine Johnson, Upaya Sangha • Tucson AZ, USA
Coast and City Sangha • South Australia
Jonathan Page, Bluegum Sangha • Sydney, Australia
Kookaburra Sangha • inner-west Sydney, Australia
Linda Modaro, Sati Sangha lead teacher • Santa Monica CA, USA
Mike Slott, New York Insight member • Montclair NJ, USA
One Heart Sangha, Ingrid Miroir de Joie Roelofs • Arnhem, Netherlands
Paul Wielgus, Back to the Roots sangha • Bath, UK
Peck Yee Tan & Christopher Minson • Ashland OR, USA
Secular Dharma Community • Vienna, Austria
Sydney Insight Meditators • Sydney, Australia
Tricia Searcy • Sierra Madre CA, USA
White Heron Sangha & Sati Sangha • San Luis Obispo CA, USA

The Tuwhiri Project is grateful for ongoing support from Aotearoa Buddhist Education Trust.